Health Forensics

© Copyright: Steven Magee 2014

Edition 1

Cover Picture: Rooms next to trees and climbing vines may be filled with electromagnetic interference (EMI) if the ground is electrified with stray voltage from the utility system. This may cause strange sickness and behavioral problems to occur in the dwellers.

Contents

Introduction

Health Forensics is developed out of the book "Toxic Health". Health Forensics presents the adverse health symptoms that were discussed in Toxic Health for those who want to diagnose biologically toxic human environments. The field of health forensics is relatively new and is currently rapidly developing. Toxic Health is an expanded version of this book and has additional information in it regarding improving human health.

Health Forensics takes a look at the modern human environment and investigates how it is impacting human health. Modern industrialized humans have adopted habits and lifestyles that did not exist even just a few years ago. Each change in lifestyle generally has a cost to pay in terms of health.

Many small changes in lifestyle can add up to large problems that are accumulating in the human mind and body and show up many years later. The modern human has adopted a lifestyle that for many comes to a crashing halt in middle age as problems such as depression, aches and pains, diabetes, high cholesterol, forgetfulness, and a loss of vitality become the norm. We are in a time like no other in human history and we are now seeing the onset of these symptoms much earlier in the human as many children are not developing correctly.

The Institute of Health Metrics and Evaluations, University of Washington, reported in 2011 that the American average life expectancy is now in decline. Ranked a lowly 38th in the world, with 1 in 8 women now getting breast cancer. In some parts of the USA the average life expectancy is just 66 years.

People have fooled themselves into thinking that by taking a cocktail of vitamin supplements and prescription pills that they will get better. The reality is that this behavior just covers up underlying problems that are getting worse. Modern society is now filled with people who have falsely pinned their hopes for the future on medications.

With approximately 50% of the USA population on prescription drugs and 10% on anti-depressants, it is clear that things are going seriously wrong with human health in the modern world.

A concerning development is that approximately 300,000 people in Sweden have registered as having Electromagnetic Hypersensitivity (EHS). EHS is caused by exposure to electrical, electronic and wireless products and Sweden is the only country that currently recognizes it as a health condition. This new epidemic in the population is predicted to keep on increasing as the use of technology gains momentum.

It does not have to be this way. After years of extensive research into human health, Health Forensics has discovered that most of these symptoms are a product of toxins that we willingly have introduced into our lifestyles and by removing them we may restore the vitality back into our lives. There is a large and extensive web of these toxins and we will look into them and identify potential health hazards.

Good health for your entire life is completely dependent on your lifestyle choices and the environments that you spend time in. Health Forensics will discuss the changes necessary to work towards a positively healthy life. Health Forensics demonstrates how to live to a good age with a healthy and painless life that is free of prescription drugs.

Diagrams and photographs are used to illustrate many of the concepts of the book. If you are reading this in black and white, descriptions of the pictures accompany them to explain the concepts. The contents of the book should be accessible to most people through the visual explanations of subjects discussed in the book.

This book is aimed at the general public, the medical profession and the engineering profession. Mathematics is avoided and the book presents the concepts of the various forms of health in a readable format to the general public. Important points are in bold font.

This book contains the very latest research on health and the human environment. It should be viewed as the current ideas and the contents are subject to review by the scientific community. The author and publisher accept no liability whatsoever for any of the contents and the book is published in the spirit of unrestricted access to the latest ideas and scientific theories in a changing world.

You should always consult with a licensed and certified medical professional on any aspects of health, sickness or disease.

"The way you think, the way you behave, the way you eat, can influence your life by 30 to 50 years."

Deepak Chopra

Basics

We know that the human cannot survive without air, water and food and these are classed as the nutrition of the human body. But if you think that is all you need to worry about, then you may eventually develop poor health. Human nutrition is far more extensive and we have a comprehensive list below:

- Air.
- Water.
- Food.
- Exercise.
- Body voltage.
- Smells.
- Temperature.
- Humidity.
- Light.
- Sleep.
- Radiation.
- Metals.
- Altitude.
- Sounds and Vibrations.
- Chemical Exposure.
- Society.

The above are all nutritional items that need to be correct in order for you to be well. It just takes some simple steps to ensure that you have an excellent chance of achieving a long and healthy life that is free of pain.

As we can see in the next table, the modern human is currently dying of three leading things:

- **Heart and circulation.**
- **Cancer.**
- **Brain issues.**

The following diagram shows the age where people start to die from these things. As can be seen, the rate of death starts significantly rising from 30 years of age onwards.

Research conducted for Health Forensics is indicating that these three leading causes of death are preventable and it just takes a lifestyle adjustment to significantly reduce the risk of succumbing to these ailments.

"Liberty is to the collective body, what health is to every individual body. Without health, no pleasure can be tasted by man; Without liberty, no happiness can be enjoyed by society."

Henry St. John

Top 15 Causes of Death in the U.S. (2007)

Rank	Ages 1–85+	Rank	Ages 1–85+	Rank	Ages 1–85+
1	Heart Disease 615,616	6	Alzheimer's Disease 74,629	11	Septicemia 34,543
2	Malignant Neoplasms 562,795	7	Diabetes Mellitus 71,373	12	Liver Disease 29,158
3	Cerebrovascular 135,814	8	Influenza and Pneumonia 52,492	13	Hypertension 23,963
4	Chronic Lower Respiratory Disease 127,875	9	Nephritis 46,304	14	Parkinson's Disease 20,056
5	Unintentional Injury 122,387	10	Suicide 34,592	15	Homicide 17,984

Data courtesy of CDC

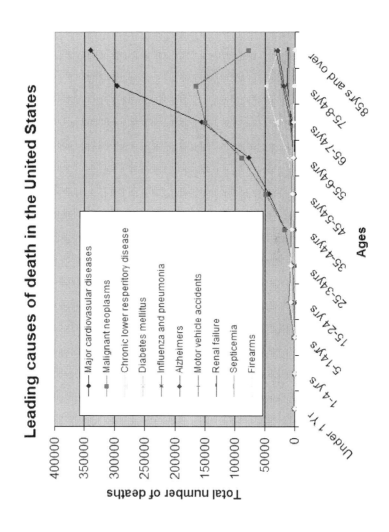

Leading causes of death in the United States

Air

Air quality is very important. Unfortunately, the industrialization of modern society has brought with it problems in air quality on a global scale. The air composition today has never existed in all of human history and it is getting worse every year. The addiction of using the air for dumping gases into by the modern human is having far reaching consequences for all life on the planet.

Indoor air can be made toxic by the use of household chemicals. Some seemingly innocent chemical products may have the ability to make you ill. Just leaving a bucket of household cleaner in the home for several days may fill the home with particles that you cannot sense. You will just notice that you are starting to get ill. It is important to use cleaning products only for short periods of time and in well ventilated spaces. Throw away any mixed products after you are done with cleaning.

Carbon monoxide poisoning can be an issue and it is odorless. This generally comes from sources of flames, such as gas heaters and fireplaces. Typically it comes from a blocked flue where the gasses come into the home instead of escaping to the outdoors. It can come from a garage if you have the car running too long in there. The symptoms to look for are:

- Headache.
- Dizziness.
- Nausea.
- Flu-like symptoms.
- Fatigue.
- Shortness of breath on exertion.
- Impaired judgment.

- Chest pain.

- Confusion.

- Depression.

- Hallucinations.

- Agitation.

- Vomiting.

- Abdominal pain.

- Drowsiness.

- Visual changes.

- Fainting.

- Seizure.

- Memory problems.

- Walking problems.

Air conditioners may have very good air quality in winter when they burn air to heat it. This draws fresh air into the home. They may have very poor air quality in the summertime when no air is drawn into the home due to cooling. ASHRAE (American Society of Heating, Refrigerating and Air Conditioning Engineers) recommends that 20 cubic feet per minute (CFM) of fresh air per person be drawn into a building for good air quality. You may need to install a fresh air vent in order to achieve this.

The top thing you can do to improve your indoor air quality is to ventilate the home to the outside air by opening the windows. Even if it is a hot or cold day, at least one window in your home should be opened slightly to allow air exchanges to take place.

So how can we gauge the progression of air pollution? The answer turns out to be relatively easy. Humans have been painting sunsets and moon-sets for hundreds of years in their artwork. Fortunately, much of this artwork has been kept in pristine condition and is available to view.

When reviewing the artwork of sunsets and moon-sets, we see that the orange and red colors appear to be a relatively modern phenomenon. Prior to this, they did not appear to be orange or red, they were relatively white.

Evidence of atmospheric pollution will be at its peak when the Sun or the Moon is near to the horizon. This is due to the radiation from these objects passing through the thickest part of the atmosphere. This is called "high air mass" in the scientific community. The radiation is subjected to the most atmospheric filtration at this time. Air mass is 1 when the Sun or Moon is at zenith and down at the horizon it is approximately 38. This means that the radiation receives 38 times more atmospheric filtration at sunset or moon-set.

Pollution causes the visible light to turn orange or red due to the filtering effects of pollution on this light. The more pollution there is, the redder it will look. This can be seen on the Island of Hawaii where the Kilauea volcano is erupting and pumping out gasses into the environment. The sunsets on this island are red, like the color of blood.

This is a problem near the poles, due to the Sun being lower in the sky. The sunlight is subjected to much more filtration by the atmosphere for longer periods of time. This may be unhealthy for people who live nearer to the poles.

Filtering solar radiation with air pollution is a bad idea.

A good example of pollution in the atmosphere is on the cover of my first book "Solar Photovoltaic Design for Residential, Commercial and Utility Systems" which is shown in the next picture. This picture was taken from the summit of Kitt Peak National Observatory in Sells, Arizona. At an elevation of approximately 6,875 feet, we can see an orange sunset. This sunset several hundred years ago probably would have been a white sunset. Orange and red sunsets are characteristic of a polluted atmosphere. Viewing the midday Sun through smoke also produces an orange or red view of it.

Atmospheric Solar Filtering at Sunset

The orange sunset from Kitt Peak at 6,875 feet.

The next picture shows the effects of atmospheric pollution on the Sun. As you can see, it is a distorted view of the Sun. It is interesting that smoking causes cancer. Could it be that smokers are having cancer induced into them by the same effects as air pollution creates with solar radiation?

To ensure that you have good air quality in your home, you should check that you have a set of vents that allow air to come in from the outside of the home. One should be about one foot from the floor and the other should be about one foot from the ceiling on the opposite side of the home. This is to ensure that a cross flow of fresh, outdoor air is allowed to circulate within the home. The vents do not have to be large, but they should permit a fresh air exchange to occur continually within the home.

Outside your home, you should have a garden with lots of trees and plants. Trees and plants purify the air, helping to create the correct composition of air for the human.

"Our most basic common link is that we all inhabit this planet. We all breathe the same air. We all cherish our children's future. And we are all mortal."

John F. Kennedy

Atmospheric Pollution

Atmospheric pollution can cause Sun filtering and interference effects.

Water

You would think that water is one of the most understood subjects of human health, but it is not. This is evidenced by the many types of bottled water that are available at the supermarket. Water is marketed as mineral, reverse osmosis, steam distilled, distilled, vitamin, electrolyte, and so on. **In this chapter we will look into the inside and outside human water. Inside water is what you drink and outside water is what you bathe in. You will be surprised at how important water is for the human and also the ticking time bomb that you may create by not using the correct type of water.**

Today, human survival on the Earth is almost completely dependent on the water tables around the world. Unfortunately, they are running out. Each year the water level is dropping and they are not being replenished. Instead, the trapped water is being released into the atmosphere where it is staying as water vapor.

This is a major problem for ground level solar radiation. Invisible water vapor appears to be raising the ground level solar radiation by lensing and interfering with the solar radiation from the Sun. This seems to have an effect in killing off some of the coral reefs in the oceans and possibly making some species of plants head towards extinction. The human race may already be heading down this route as well.

The only way that our planet can support the huge number of humans is due to the pumping of the underground water table. To stop using it means that we have to reduce the population size naturally at the earliest opportunity.

Trapped water is dead water. It may not have seen the surface of the Earth for a very long time. This is in contrast to river water that supports life within it. Trapped water has a very high mineral content associated with it. As

it starts to run out, it is highly likely that it will become toxic to humans.

Let us take a look at the different types of natural water:

- Rain is solar irradiated, radio frequency exposed, de-mineralized water with added nitrogen.
- River water is solar irradiated, grounded, mineralized water.
- Spring water is grounded, mineralized water.
- Sea water is solar irradiated, grounded, mineralized, high sodium water.

The human was drinking fresh river and spring water up until recently. Now let us see what the industrialized world calls water:

- Treated water.
- Particle filtered water.
- Carbon filtered water.
- Softened water.
- Reverse osmosis water.
- Steam distilled water.

Each of these is completely different from the other. It is somewhat ironic that the correct water to drink is the very first one, which is also known as "municipal water". It has plenty of minerals which the human body needs to extract from the water for the body to function correctly. It is unfortunate that fluoride may be added to the water supply which removes the choice of having it or not. Fluoride is a byproduct of the fertilizer industry and may

contain other toxic chemicals in it due to the way that it is produced.

The problem with filtered water is that you remove many of the particles that are present in it that the human body would either naturally use or reject. Filtered water may remove some of the organic nutrients that are actually useful to your body. You should remember that your body is equipped to drink natural untreated water, it has been doing it for thousands of years. You already possess an excellent water filtration system in your body, so this step at home is not needed.

Carbon filtering takes a lot of the chemical content out of the water. You may want to consider doing this if your water is known to be polluted but all municipal water has passed stringent tests to come into your home. You should only be carbon filtering water if you suspect that it needs to be done. Otherwise you are reducing the nutrient content of the water that you are feeding your body.

Softened water is a bad idea. Water softeners use a chemical ion exchange to change out calcium and magnesium ions for sodium ions. Sodium is salt, so you are changing your water from mineralized water to sodium water. You may get ill in the long term if you drank and bathed in this water. On the inside it is lacking essential minerals that your body needs and it has added sodium. On the outside it will start to strip minerals from your skin through osmosis. Chemically softened water does not occur in nature and you would be wise to avoid this type of water. If you were to water your plants with this water, then they may actually show stress and possibly die off. Some people who drink, bathe and shower in ion exchanged water react to it and will show skin rashes or itchy skin.

Water softeners are sold to people on the basis that it is better for washing clothes in and also protects your plumbing. The reality is that you may actually damage your plumbing, as softened water is unstable and wants to absorb minerals and it will do so by trying to extract them from your plumbing system. The same effect takes place in your body when you drink or bathe in it. You would not want to be exposing yourself to water that has extracted chemicals from your plumbing system.

Reverse osmosis water is promoted by many as being the same as rainwater. This is an incorrect statement as it is not the same as rainwater, it is just highly filtered and purified mineral water. It still does contain some contaminants, just in much lower numbers. Reverse osmosis is an extremely wasteful process with some units throwing way over 90% of the water to get less than 10% of usable water. It consumes a lot of energy as it needs pressure to push the water through the reverse osmosis filter membrane.

I have heard people call reverse osmosis water "*the best detergent know to man*" due to its ability to clean things. The reason why it is so good at cleaning is because it is unstable. The water is so clean that it wants to absorb the minerals around it to get back into the stable mineralized state. It will do the same with your body on both the inside and outside. You should avoid reverse osmosis water if you value your health.

Steam distilled water is probably the most expensive water that you can buy. It is what you are recommended to use in your steam iron to stop calcium deposits building up. This is the water that is most like rainwater. It is the purest man-made water generally available and I recommend that you only use it for the industrial purposes that it is recommended for. You should not be drinking or bathing in distilled water of any type long term.

Bottled water can be any of the above types. There is so much confusion regarding the labeling of bottled water that I recommend that you avoid it. Water cooler water that is in many offices has the same issues and I would recommend that you use municipal water for drinking due to the mineral content of it that your body requires. One of the major problems with bottled water is that it generally comes in plastic bottles. These bottles contain chemicals that can leach into the water over time and you may find yourself drinking some of the chemicals of the plastic as well as the water. These leached chemicals may impact your health later in life.

Softened, reverse osmosis and steam distilled water are all forms of de-mineralized water. It was shown back in the 1960's that the body actually appears to need hard water

so that it can extract the minerals from it. **Lack of these minerals was found to cause heart arrhythmia. Many studies of hard water areas have found much lower incidences in cardiovascular diseases, cancer, respiratory diseases, diabetes and other health problems. When it comes to water, hard water is always your best choice for the human body.**

Naturally occurring soft water does not have sodium ions as the chemical version does. It is soft because it is low on mineral content.

Drinking de-mineralized water regularly is known to cause acute health problems. This is due to calcium and magnesium being essential to the human body. The problems linked to low mineral intake are hypertension, coronary heart disease, gastric and duodenal ulcers, chronic gastritis, goitre, pregnancy complications and complications in infants.

We mentioned carbon filtering earlier. This is how trees and plants purify the water. A tree will absorb the water, store it, and slowly release it through its roots into the environment. Trees and plants are made of carbon, hence the carbon filtering that is prevalent in the water treatment industry. Water gets further filtration and mineralization through the soil before it gets into streams and rivers.

Swimming pools are an issue due to the chemicals that they contain. Every time that you swim in a swimming pool, you will be exposed to these. It is a well known problem in the industry and "Swimming Pool Cancer Risk" is extensively documented.

"Stray voltage" can be an issue around water and we will look into this later in the book.

Microwaved water is known for its toxicity. People have watered plants with microwaved water and have noticed that they tend to die! This is because the structure of the water has changed. Water structure is well known to be altered with light, sound, temperature, radio frequency, magnetic and electric fields. Some types of structuring are known for their health benefits, while others may make you sick. Human blood is 92%

water and you need to be careful how you let it be structured by external influences.

This is somewhat disturbing, given that the utilities are now installing high powered radio frequency transmitting devices onto domestic water supplies in the USA. Commonly called Smart/AMR/AMI utility meters, the utilities are now structuring the water that they are delivering to your home. The long term health effects of drinking such water is currently unknown at the time of writing.

Carbonated soft drinks should be avoided due to the carbonic acid that may damage the bones in the long term. Tea and coffee can act as diuretics and dehydrate you. The caffeine in them can upset your sleep cycles.

Testing of the various kinds of water led to the understanding that hot tea that had cooled had particularly beneficial effects on plants. It appeared to create resistance to radio frequency exposures. A daily pot of hot tea is likely to be beneficial to the human due to the nutrients that it contains. Outside of a daily pot of tea, you should be simply drinking municipal water. Drinking tea exclusively is known to create long term health problems. The radio frequency exposed, tea drinking Dieffenbachia plant is shown in the next picture alongside one that is only being given Tucson faucet water.

Tea Appears to Create Radiation Resistance

Watering a Dieffenbachia plant with hot tea that had cooled greatly improved its growth patterns in a radio frequency field when contrasted to the smaller and deformed Dieffenbachia plant that only got Tucson faucet water.

Gardeners have noticed that rainwater invigorates plants and it is likely due to this water being infused with nitrogen from the air and radio frequency exposed. Plants prefer to be watered through their leaves by this naturally treated rain water. Watering a plant with municipal water through its roots appears to be one of the reasons why you have to fertilize them.

A company called Vi Aqua (www.viaqua.com) markets a device that irradiates water with radio frequency at 27 megahertz. They claim that it extends the life of cut flowers and acts like fertilizer for plants, increasing the growth mass. They state the following effects have been observed in plants watered with radio frequency irradiated municipal water:

- **30% - 40% increase in crop size and yield.**
- **More disease-resistant.**
- **Require far less fertilizer.**
- **Need one third less water.**
- **Will thrive in poor soil.**
- **Taste better.**
- **Longer shelf life.**
- **Increases the solubility of nutrients in the water.**
- **Improves the quality of the plant and its lush appearance.**
- **Improves roots development.**
- **Optimizes the use of water by increasing its efficiency.**
- **Significant de-scaling effect in pipes and nozzles.**

What they have done is take an effect that is found in thunderstorms and apply it to groundwater. As can be seen, irradiating municipal water with radio frequency can accelerate growth and extend life. We also know that irradiating water with other frequencies can have detrimental effects.

A place where we find water in the human is in the amniotic fluid in the womb. Irradiating the womb with strange man-made frequencies would be expected to have an effect. Today, many women cannot give birth naturally to their babies because they are too big! Of those that do give birth naturally, they have a tendency to rip the vaginal canal due to the large size of the baby. It is quite possible that babies are significantly larger today because of man-made electromagnetic interference exposures! It may be the reason why they no longer fit into the birth canal in many cases. There is evidence in the historical records that indicates that birth weights increased after the introduction of the telegraph and electricity to the cities. The correct human birth weight appears to be in the 4 to 5 pound range. We know that delivering an oversized baby does damage to the birth canal and it is not recommended for good female health. Unfortunately, 6 to 10 pound babies appears to be a product of modern society.

Aaron Alexis, Navy Yard shooting suspect, thought people followed him with a microwave machine. He was actually correct in his assessment, as wondering around a modern city has you in high-powered microwave fields. You could be standing next to a high-powered cell phone microwave transmitter system and not even know it! Children in cities are noted for their accelerating development into puberty and irradiation of their body water by unnatural high-powered man-made radio waves is likely involved in this process.

You should avoid purchasing food and water from shops that are near to transmitter systems or that have wireless networking. It is likely that the food and water will have been structured and may have long term toxic effects to the human.

To sum up, the preference for good human health is to be drinking water that has been irradiated naturally by nature, not mankind.

"Water is the driving force of all nature."
Leonardo da Vinci

Food

Food is very well understood by humanity, but they just keep on ignoring the advice and eating foods from sources that should be avoided. Clearly a diet of fast food, genetically modified food, processed food, preserved food, and so on may make you ill eventually.

Organically grown fresh food is what you should be eating. The mix of food is generally incorrect and you should be eating a diet that consists mainly of fruits and vegetables. Meat and fish should probably comprise of less than 10% of your diet content. Fruits and vegetables are known for their antioxidant properties that prevent illness and disease.

Here is what you should be aiming for:

- **47% Vegetables.**
- **47% Fruits.**
- **3% Fish.**
- **3% Meat.**

You should realize that it is just a guide and feel free to indulge once a week in your favorite foods. A handful of nuts daily is a good habit, assuming you are not allergic to them.

The diagram on the next page shows the plant based food diet.

Plant Based Food Diet

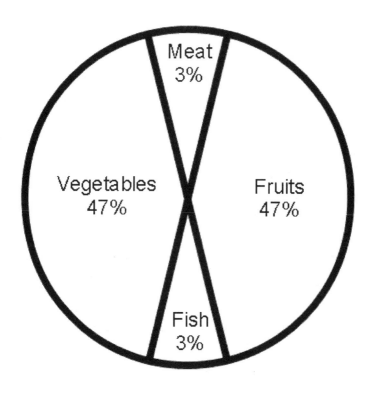

The adoption by many people of the "Atkins Diet" revealed problems in eating a diet that is largely comprised of meat. As the years passed, more health conditions were linked to this diet of high protein and fat intake. Some of these were:

- Coronary heart disease.
- Bad breath.
- Constipation.
- Dizziness.
- Headaches.
- Pregnancy issues.

Dairy is an unnatural food that humans should not be consuming. If you look at nature, there is no animal that consumes breast milk as an adult. The human is the only animal to do this, and it does it by drinking the breast milk of an entirely different species!

Calcium has long been quoted by the milk industry as an important aspect of health. Hard water and plant based foods contains all of the calcium that you will ever need as an adult! Instead of being led by biased advertising from the milk industry, you should follow what nature does:

Milk products should be avoided as an adult.

Modern humans have fat in common with diary animals. When you look at the fat cells of a modern human, they are the same color as the fat cells of diary cows. They are both yellow in color. This is in contrast to the fat on wild animals which is white. Both the modern human and the dairy cows lead similar lifestyles and it should be of no surprise to see that they share this feature. The reasons for this may be:

- Eating incorrect food.
- Exposure to the electrical system.
- Life under artificial lights.
- An indoor lifestyle.
- Disconnection from nature.
- Exposure to pollution.
- Lack of exercise.
- Loss of DC body voltage.

As people have started to realize, the modern human is a different creature from the human that lives a natural lifestyle in harmony with nature. People who are living in harmony with nature generally have little fat and it is white in color. You can tell the health of a person simply by the color of their fat. This fat effect was noted by Kevin Patterson in his book "Consumption".

Avoid being a fussy eater and eat everything on your plate. Use spices and sauces to give your food variety. Avoid having the same meal twice in one week. Pay attention to food that does not agree with your digestive system and may cause mouth or intestinal irritation to occur. Such foods should be avoided.

Being green on the inside is known to have protective properties to the human mind and body and you should aim for the majority of your diet to come from plant sources. NASA extensively uses fruit and vegetable based supplements to prevent cancer from occurring from Space radiation in the astronauts on the International Space Station.

"One cannot think well, love well, sleep well, if one has not dined well."

Virginia Woolf

30

Exercise

NASA has known for decades that if the astronauts do not exercise for approximately two hours per day when in Space that they will get sick. The top job an astronaut must do is exercise daily when on board the International Space Station! Most modern humans now live in alien environments that are more comparable to Space than nature. Modern human environments are commonly devoid of trees and greenery. Instead concrete, paints and man-made materials predominate. The radiation levels have greatly increased with the advent of electricity and the associated products. Homes and workplaces are filled with electrical, electronic and wireless products. The environment in general is now heavily contaminated with wireless radiation that was not there even just a few years ago. The environment is overloaded with many wireless radiation sources.

To be healthy in modern society, you must adopt the behaviors of an astronaut!

NASA knows that sedate exercising, such as walking, does not work for the astronauts on the International Space Station. The exercise that they must do to stay in good health is vigorous exercise that strengthens the muscles throughout the body and makes them sweat! It is a tough job being an astronaut!

You are the equivalent of an astronaut living in modern society and you must copy what the astronauts are doing on the International Space Station in order to maintain good health. Daily high activity exercise is a must.

In order to do this I identified a workout DVD called "Supreme 90 Day System". The reason why I chose this DVD was because it was affordable, had great reviews, it converted fat

31

to muscle mass and needed only a balance ball and dumb bells to perform the exercises at home. The exercises consists of ten routines of less than an hour each. They are relatively easy to do and get you sweating by the end of the routine.

I was quite shocked at how rapidly I saw the changes occurring. By the end of ten days, I had lost 6 pounds and my hunger had subsided. I was looking better and feeling great after the workouts. Clothes started to fit well and my health was improving. After twenty days my weight had stabilized, my muscle strength had greatly increased and the workouts were becoming routine and enjoyable. By thirty days my stamina had developed and I was able to fully perform each exercise routine.

It confirmed what I had been suspecting for quite some time, that walking is not really an effective exercise. I had been regularly walking for approximately an hour per day for exercise during the previous few years. When I started the workout DVD I was shocked at how unfit I had become!

When you are not exercising effectively every day, a process called "Muscle Atrophy" starts to take place. Every muscle that is not being used reduces in size. The process can be extreme in people who have had limbs immobilized through accidents or injury. Muscle atrophy is a wasting condition and it is highly undesirable to let your body go into this process.

Once the body has atrophied, you will become vulnerable to many conditions. This is because the human body was never meant to be in this condition. It is highly unnatural. The human spent thousands of years being active daily through hunting and gathering and your ancestors were really fit people! Modern society has brought with it sedentary lifestyles for the masses that are extremely unnatural. When man was a hunter gatherer, these atrophied humans would have been easy prey for any predator and atrophied humans were probably sparse. Muscle atrophy is not a natural state in the natural world and you should avoid entering into this condition.

I appeared to enter this condition when I started to work in desk jobs. This coincided with showing breathing difficulties and chest pains at the age of 37 when I was jogging in 2007. I did not know it at the time, but I had developed radiation sickness from working at high altitudes, sitting near to electrical rooms, exposure to electrical, electronic and wireless radiation emissions, and man-made ultraviolet light from florescent lights. Needless to say, once I started showing serious health conditions during exercise, I stopped jogging!

When I was researching why so many people were reporting reactions to radio waves, which is commonly called "Electromagnetic Hypersensitivity", muscle atrophy was one of my suspicions for it. Out of my family, I am the only one who does not exercise and I was the only person who was showing the sensitivity to wireless radiation. It appears that once the body has atrophied, then increased sensitivity to wireless radiation should be expected. This is because the electrical characteristics of the human body have changed. Muscle has very different electrical characteristics to fat.

You can buy devices that measure the fat content of the body using the principles of electrical conductivity. A fat human has a very different electrical conductivity to a muscular human. As such, the electrical properties of an atrophied human are very different to those of a muscular human. The electronic devices are commonly called "Body Fat Monitors" and use the principle of "Bioelectric Impedance Analysis (BIA)".

It appears that muscle atrophy puts the human into a zombie-like state that is unnatural. The body is not dead, but it is not fully alive either. This opens up the human for biological attack on many fronts. The natural world defines an atrophied human as weak and will target it. Your body was never meant to function in the natural world in an atrophied state.

Fortunately, muscle atrophy is easily avoidable and it simply requires that you do effective strength exercises daily. If you want to be healthy, you need to be in good physical condition with toned muscles. Human resources departments have known for a long time that people who look healthy and keep fit generally are the healthiest employees!

It is in your interest to be fit and strong. The health benefits far outweigh the time that it takes to keep yourself toned. Exercising will keep you in harmony with the natural world. Skin that is made to sweat eliminates toxins from the body in the process and cleanses the human. Exercise that makes you hot throughout is raising your core temperature and changes the cellular system environment in a positive way.

Muscle clearly has electromagnetic shielding properties for the human body. Physical exercise that causes the brain to move around will improve the supporting structure to the brain and may well increase its resistance to man-made electromagnetic radiation exposures. After six months of building muscle mass I can now confirm that muscle mass creates increased tolerance to biologically harmful radiation sources.

After six months of vigorous exercising to build muscle, my body is now lean. I combined this technique with creating a DC voltage on the human body and this has coincided with no longer observing the adverse reactions that I was displaying regarding continuous radio frequency exposures at my home. We will discuss the creation of the DC body voltage in the next chapter.

The elderly and infirm are typically in some state of atrophication. Unfortunately, babies and many modern children are in the atrophied state and this makes them vulnerable to radiation exposures. The environment that the next generation are being raised in is very unnatural and is hostile to atrophied youngsters. We will look into the rise of Autism in the children later in the book.

"Those who think they have no time for bodily exercise will sooner or later have to find time for illness."

Edward Stanley

Body Voltage

Most people associate direct current (DC) voltage with batteries. It has a constant voltage that does not change over time. What most people do not know is that the human is supposed to have a DC voltage on its body relative to its feet. This voltage is generated from both the atmosphere and nutritional intake.

Atmospheric energy has direct current in it and it has a voltage gradient that is positive relative to the ground in clear conditions. In cloudy conditions it is negative for the first couple of miles above the ground and that then changes to positive polarity as you go higher into the atmosphere. Close to the ground the voltage increase is between 1 to 19 volts per foot. Flying kites with conductive strings will expose you to this atmospheric voltage, as will helium balloons with long conductive strings. Higher up in the atmosphere, the voltage increases by approximately 30 volts per foot.

All living organisms that stand tall on the ground are subjected to this DC voltage and this is evidenced in the following pictures.

The Dieffenbachia grows well regardless of if the voltage is positive or negative 1.5 volts on its stem relative to the roots. It indicates that the atmospheric DC voltage polarity may reverse in nature over time. It seems that the atmospheric DC voltage in my area has changed, which is very concerning!

If the DC voltage gets too high, then the Dieffenbachia plant starts to show stress. 9 volts positive polarity on the stem appears to cause growth defects (shown) and seems more harmful than 9 volts negative stem polarity that seems to stunt growth and corrodes the metal alligator clip.

My plants are grown in high radiation fields that appear to come from radio frequency transmitting utility meters and three cell phone towers that are between 600-700 meters from my home. The Dieffenbachia's all deform at my home regardless of where they are grown at on my property. As we can see in the plants, we can restore the normal growth patterns by applying a DC voltage to them. The voltage has to be kept to the correct level, otherwise stresses will show up if too high or too low. Applying a DC voltage between the soles of the feet of the human and the upper body may have applications in the field of human health. This is shown in the next diagram.

I have been experimenting with putting the human mind and body into a DC electric field during sleep. I have a large sheet of conductive aluminum foil attached to the 10 feet high ceiling above the bed and a large sheet of conductive aluminum foil on the floor under the bed to effect this. The upper sheet is connected to the negative terminal of a battery and the lower sheet is connected to the positive terminal. This can be seen in the following photograph.

The upper sheet is akin to the tree canopy which is known to have a DC voltage on it. A company called Voltree Power (www.voltreepower.com) is developing the use of tree voltage to power electronic systems and has extensively researched the DC voltage of trees.

The feet are connected together through being in contact with the conductive ground and are earthed (grounded). The mind and body are walking around in a DC voltage field. That DC voltage will energize the mind and body and the lack of it may make the human sick.

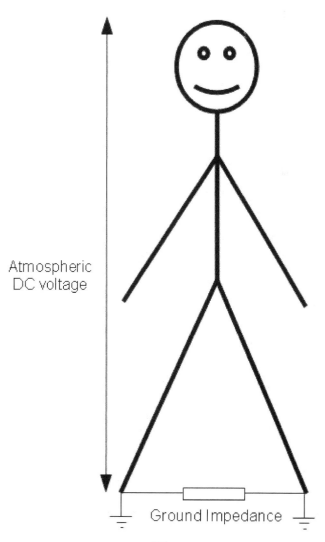

Human Electrical Model

The upper and lower sheets of aluminum foil are the same size as the bed. The DC voltage on the conductive sheets will set up a DC voltage field between them with a small flow of energy that should pass through the human sleeping in the bed. This is currently an unproven experimental health technique that may have unknown side effects. I call this technique: "Electromagnetic Sandwich"

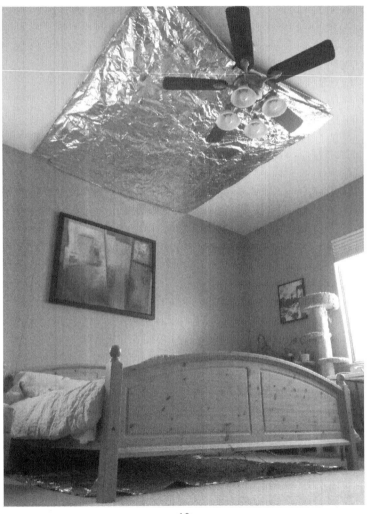

I started testing the Electromagnetic Sandwich with a 9 volt battery which should give approximately 2 volts of a negative atmospheric voltage exposure to my mind and body during sleep. The atmospheric voltage gradient between the floor sheet and the ceiling negative sheet is -0.9 volt DC per foot. I could definitely feel the difference when I was sleeping and headaches and muscle weakness showed up after about a week of testing. I changed the battery to 1.5 volt DC and found that this was much more agreeable to human health and the health problems cleared up. 1.5 volts DC appears to be more comparable to what you find on the tree canopy. I may adjust the DC voltage later, depending on what I find with long term testing.

It is interesting that the human health difference in the DC voltage exposures matches what I saw in the Dieffenbachia plants. Exposure to a very low DC voltage that is comparable to a single DC battery cell appears healthy for biological systems and 9 volts DC stresses them.

My initial assessment of the Electromagnetic Sandwich health technique was that the occasional daytime fatigue that I was experiencing significantly reduced. I find this very concerning, as it indicates that a DC atmospheric voltage is missing at my home that is required for both good plant health and good human health. It appears that people who suffer from Electromagnetic Hypersensitivity may be reacting to this loss of atmospheric DC voltage. They appear to be the electromagnetic radiation equivalent of the "Coalminers canary" and it is very foolish to ignore the health symptoms that these many people are reporting. They are very clearly reacting to unnatural man-made electromagnetic radiation conditions.

I further developed the Electromagnetic Sandwich technique for daytime use. It is easily implemented using an anti-static wrist strap and an anti-static mat. This is shown in the next picture. For those of you on the go, you can wear an anti-static heel strap and an anti-static wrist strap and just put the 1.5 volt DC battery in your pocket. Keep the cables as short as possible and it is preferable to use straight cables as opposed to the coiled cables shown in the picture. Long cables and cable coils act as antenna systems and will put strange frequencies onto the DC voltage that may lead to electromagnetic hypersensitivity.

These health techniques are experimental and have unknown side effects at the time of writing. The DC voltages may require adjusting to higher or lower levels and will be person dependent due to the impedance of the fat to muscle ratio. They may need to only be applied for short periods rather than continuous use. This is a developing area of research that is very new and there are a lot of unknowns currently.

If you choose to implement them, you should be under qualified and competent medical supervision and discontinue the techniques if adverse health symptoms show up. You would be assuming any and all risks using these health techniques.

When I discontinued the application of -1.5 volts DC from a single cell battery, I did develop a large withdrawal headache that slowly subsided over a few days. While I did initial testing with a negative body polarity, I currently recommend that a positive body polarity be used in the Electromagnetic Sandwich, as this appears to be what the body naturally produces, as we will see later.

Experimenting with wearing an anti-static strap on my wrist that is connected to the negative terminal of a 1.5 volt DC battery. The positive terminal is connected to an anti-static mat that my bare feet rest on. This creates a DC voltage gradient across my body that is similar to what nature does. Both the mat and the wrist strap have 1,000,000 ohm resistors built into them.

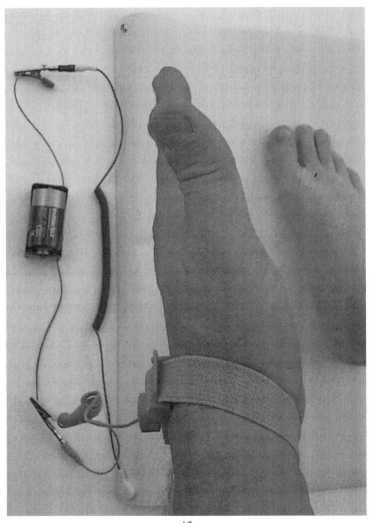

Zinc batteries are in common use, most disposable batteries that you buy for your products are zinc based. There are three types of zinc batteries and these are zinc-carbon, zinc-chloride and zinc-air. This is significant because the human body is made predominantly of carbon, through the lungs it absorbs air and chloride is salt that is present in the blood. So if you put zinc into the human body, you essentially create a zinc battery! It is widely recognized that the human mind and body functions on electricity and zinc is likely a key factor in this electrical functioning. It is clear from the plant experiments that wireless radiation is interfering with the DC voltage biological effects.

Natural sources of zinc are meat, poultry, diary products, beans, whole grains and nuts. You can create the zinc battery effect in the human body through zinc supplementation. You need to be careful with zinc supplementation as it may prevent copper absorption and you can overdose. Low level overdosing shows up as gastrointestinal symptoms and vomiting, severe overdosing can cause anemia, fever and central nervous system effects.

50% of zinc in the human body is found within the muscles. For this reason, you should ensure that you are muscular when in abnormal electromagnetic fields that are characteristic of modern cities. Muscles are the zinc batteries of the human body! Given that electromagnetic fields appear to deplete the zinc levels, you should be supplementing with zinc to replenish the levels when in a city environment.

All batteries are made from an electrolyte and at least two electrodes. The lemon battery is a good example of this. Inserting a piece of copper and a piece of zinc into a lemon creates the lemon battery. The lemon battery will generate a voltage of approximately 0.9 volts. This voltage can be increased by using magnesium in place of zinc. Magnesium and copper electrodes in lemons will generate approximately 1.6 volts DC. Many metals can be used to create the lemon battery, as can many fruits and vegetables.

The human is an electrolyte. The addition of metals to the human body will create the DC voltage effect. In 2013

I started to dose the human body with metal supplements to create metal electrodes within the body. The addition of salt increases the effectiveness of the body electrolyte. The voltage that I obtained after several weeks of dosing was in the range of +0.4 to +0.8 volts. These measurements were between the grounded feet and the tip of the finger or between the grounded feet the metal bridge in my mouth. The metal bridge always had the highest voltage and was approximately +0.2 volts higher than the finger tip. It was typical to see +0.5 volts on the finger tip and +0.7 volts on the metal dental bridge, relative to the grounded feet. These voltages were measured with an Amprobe 5XP-A multimeter.

The current produced was low and was about 5 microamps between the grounded feet and the finger tip. The current from the metal bridge to the grounded feet was much higher at up to 49 microamps. The voltage of the human body was always positive relative to the feet and this matches the atmospheric voltage in clear conditions. Given that the atmospheric voltage reverses in cloudy conditions, it may be related to the reason why so many people show depressive mood disorders in cloudy cities.

In nature, you would get the minerals and salts through your diet. In particular, coastal residents would be getting much higher levels of salts from their ocean based diet of fish and sea vegetables. The coastal Mediterranean lifestyle is associated with good health and is likely related to the optimum dosing of the body with metals and electrolytes through their diet.

It is likely that the body has the ability to be charged from the DC voltage in the atmosphere. In this situation, the grounded feet would form one plate of the battery and the skin of the body would form the other plate. Hair on the body likely increases the surface area of the skin to increase the effectiveness of the connection to the DC voltage in the atmosphere. This connection to the atmospheric DC voltage may facilitate the correct chemical composition of the electrolyte of the human body. Without the atmospheric DC

voltage, the human may slowly fall into sickness and perhaps onto disease and premature death.

The DC atmospheric voltage is heavily interfered with by radio frequencies, tall structures and towers, and it appears to be either significantly reduced or missing at my home. It has been noticed that corrosion is accelerated near to transmitter systems and it is likely related to this effect. Corrosion is strongly tied to DC galvanic effects. As we now know, reduction or loss of DC atmospheric voltage equates to accelerated corrosion, plant retardation and poor human health. It may also be related to climate change and extreme weather events.

As such, I have been experimenting with the following supplements to create the battery effect in the human body:

- Cobalt (B-12).
- Copper.
- Iron.
- Magnesium.
- Salt.
- Zinc.

The plagues of our children are Autism and Attention Deficit Disorder (ADD). Doctors have found that the following supplements reduce symptoms in these children:

Autism: Cobalt (B-12).

ADD: Magnesium and zinc.

The doctors who supplement children with these are unlikely to realize that they are creating a DC voltage on the human body. It is likely that the presence of the DC voltage is reducing these conditions.

When applying a DC voltage between the foot and the wrist, a reaction occurred in my urine. It started to smell like a strong chemical, similar to WD-40. I was concerned that this may have been a reaction to the battery and it was one of the reasons why I switched over to creating the DC voltage with supplements. After ceasing to apply the battery voltage, the chemical smelling urine disappeared after approximately one week. It reappeared shortly after supplementing for DC voltage. The chemical smelling urine lasted for a few months until finally reverting back to its normal smell. I am assuming that the DC voltage created a reaction in the body that was causing elimination of a stored substance that currently remains unidentified.

Another source of the above metal supplements is multivitamins. Multivitamins are a minefield and you should not go out and buy them unless you know what supplements that you require. Many people have made themselves sick by using the wrong multivitamin formulation. The next time you are in the supermarket, pick some different brands of multivitamins up and read the supplement information. They will likely all be very different from each other.

If you are suffering from radio frequency exposures, then the electrolytes and metals appear to offer good resistance to them. Given the large scale deployment of radio frequency producing devices over the last decade, it is likely that you may have conditions that are related to these exposures. Accelerated metal corrosion has been widely observed near to radio frequency transmitters and it is probable that it also corrodes the metals within the human body. Reduction of the body metals may result in a reduction of the DC body voltage which may lead to sickness.

When supplementing, I would recommend that you check out the reviews for the supplements that you are planning on taking to ensure that people are having success with them. Everyone is different and what works for one may not work for another. Different brands may use different sources for their supplements and comparable supplements may have contrasting effects due to manufacturing differences. You should consult with your doctor regarding the correct supplements to take.

I currently supplement daily with the following to create the DC voltage on the human body:

B-12: 500 mcg

Copper: 2 mg

Iron: 25 mg

Magnesium: 250 mg

Zinc: 19 mg

Salt: 1,000 mg

Comparable formulations may be found in some multivitamins. I have found that my overall health has increased since supplementing and this is in line with the DC voltage and currents that have appeared during that time. Supplementing with other additional metals may increase the beneficial effects of the DC voltage. You will need to discuss an appropriate supplementation dose with your doctor if you choose to do this.

A word of warning: I originally took the metal supplements separately every two hours during the daytime. So the first metal was taken at 08:00, the second at 10:00, the third at 12:00, and so on until I had taken all of the different supplements for the day. This had the very interesting effect of making my brain functioning go very weird, confused and forgetful! It appeared that I had created a DC battery within the intestines!!! Striping of the intestines with different metals is very undesirable and matches the findings that human brain functioning and intestinal health are strongly linked. Taking all of the supplements together at breakfast remedied the brain problems.

I saw my mating cycle get triggered when taking high doses of zinc during developing the metal supplementation techniques. It was likely a reaction to the rapidly changing DC voltage levels. Too much daily zinc eventually led to a metallic taste in the mouth, runny nose, sore throat and fatigue. This led to me reducing the dosage.

I saw headaches develop initially when supplementing with salt. This was accompanied by nerve twitching. It cleared up after approximately a week.

My thyroid became sore and it was difficult to swallow during the initial few months of DC supplementation. It felt like a lump in my throat, although to the touch there was nothing there. It subsided to the just the right side of my thyroid and then eventually disappeared.

Introducing metal supplements into the human body is likely to increase the electromagnetic shielding effects. It appears that a human who is supplementing with metals becomes more resistant to radio frequency exposures.

I have tested two multivitamins that are branded "Energy". I never noticed much difference with either when compared to the supplements that I use for DC voltage. Going into rural areas, beaches and the countryside is the most effective energy supplement that I have found and this is line with the cities being filled with excessive radio frequency energy which is well known to induce fatigue into many people.

I call supplementing with electrolytes and metals:

The Electrical Chemistry of the Human

It is my conclusion that the human mind and body is essentially a single cell rechargeable battery that is charged from the atmospheric DC voltage and the Earth. When in areas where the atmospheric DC voltage is reduced or missing, the human slowly discharges and becomes sick. The human can be recharged either by going into rural areas where the atmospheric DC voltage is still intact, or by connecting a single cell battery between the soles of the feet and the wrist, or by ingesting electrolytes and a wide range of

metal supplements. Human battery discharge rates appear to increase if the person has metal implants. Human mind and body metals appear to be lost through radio frequency exposure and I call this hypothesis:

Internal Human Corrosion

Internal human corrosion that leads to the loss of human DC voltage appears to be a slow form of electrocution that may lead to premature death over many decades. It may be also caused by metal implants in the body. Self discharge of batteries typically occurs at rates of 8% to 20% per year and the human may display similar discharge rates. Discharge occurs due to internal currents within the battery. If the human is not charged daily from the atmospheric DC voltage and the ground, then complete DC discharge may eventually occur and the human essentially becomes a flat battery.

For more information on body voltage, I can recommend the following books

"Healing is Voltage" by Jerry Tennant.

"The Body Electric: Electromagnetism And The Foundation Of Life" by Robert Becker.

"We cannot hope to either understand or to manage the carbon in the atmosphere unless we understand and manage the trees and the soil too."

Freeman Dyson

Smells

One of the things that you will notice when in a forested environment are the smells! Everything around you will be releasing scents and pollen into the air. Plant scents and pollen may be essential to good human health! The nose and lungs extract the scents and pollen for use in the human body.

The other thing you will notice when you look at modern society is the large number of people who have allergies. This is not normal. Clearly, we are a species that lived in the forest until a few hundred years ago and we were not allergic to it. Allergies are a result of a modern industrial society. It is far more likely to be related to the stress placed onto the body by living in an unnatural environment.

With each change that the modern human has made to its environment, new stresses were introduced. This build up of stresses leads to a poorly functioning human. Once the human is in the poorly functioning state, it becomes prone to illness and disease. Allergies are one of the signs of this poorly functioning state.

Exposure to pollen may be needed to be in a healthy state and you should be querying why you are allergic to something that humans have lived in the presence of for thousands of years. It is most likely that something in your environment is making your body react to it. If you have gone into pollen deficiency, then the adverse reaction to the arrival of higher pollen levels is normal and the best way to deal with it is to actually increase your outdoor time in natural green environments! Your body should adjust to the presence of pollen within a few weeks.

Avoiding pollen when your body is pollen deficient is a bad idea and will only make matters worse. Unfortunately, it is very easy to become pollen deficient in a city environment with the lack of nature in the area. The sealed up, air conditioned homes just add to the problem of pollen

deficiency. Smart people keep their windows open, have plants inside, gardens outside, and spend daily outdoor time in the nearest natural green environment with trees.

Outdoor smells change with the seasons and also with humidity. You will notice that during and after rains that you will be smelling air that is infused with nature!

Modern homes are connected into sewer systems. You need to be careful with your sewer system as it has the potential to fill your home with sewer gas! Sewer gas is poisonous and explosive. If homes in your area start to mysteriously explode, it is likely that the sewer system is aging and has started to leak sewer gas into the home.

Sewer gas is generally noticeable when coming into the home from outdoors after the home has been locked up for several hours. If you enter the home and notice a strange smell, then it is likely that your sewer line is leaking somewhere inside the home. Things that can cause this are:

- Drains traps have dried out.
- Toilet drain wax seal is leaking.
- Cracked drain.
- Kitchen island vent valve is leaking.
- Dishwasher or washer needs to be run.

All drains should have water flushed through them at least twice a week to prevent them from drying out and leaking sewer gas into the home. They rely on the presence of water to seal the drain. Your washer and dishwasher should be run at least twice per week to prevent any water inside of it going moldy and emitting spores.

The guest bathroom is particularly hazardous for single people and couples. If you have guests infrequently, then the drains in that room are likely to dry out and vent the sewer system gas into your home! You should make a point of regularly going into this room and flushing all of the drains with water to ensure that they are sealed.

You should pay attention to how your home smells when entering it. It is good practice to take a big sniff of the air every time you enter the home. Strange smells should be tracked down. Low levels of sewer gas smell like rotten eggs and high levels can destroy your sense of smell. The symptoms to look for are:

- Extreme fatigue.

- Dizziness.

- Headaches.

- Irritability.

- Memory loss.

- Runny eyes.

- Runny nose.

- Excitation.

- Rapid breathing.

- Headaches.

- Seizures.

- Loss of consciousness.

- Coma.

- Death.

Out-gassing can be a problem and is noticeable around new products. Most people associate it with the new car smell. That new car smell is the products releasing gasses into the car from the chemicals that were used to make it. You generally notice out-gassing in the home whenever you bring a new item into the home, such as a new sofa or mattress. It is important to ventilate your home well

during the few weeks after introducing a new item into the home. If your home is exhibiting the new car smell, then you should have your windows open.

Out-gassing is noticeable for a few weeks after introducing a new product. Over time the product will release less gas and the new smell will slowly subside. Many products will continue to out-gas indefinitely, but the volume of gas is low that they emit. It is for this reason that you should ensure that your home has adequate outdoor ventilation installed into it to enable the out-gassing to escape into the outdoors. This is a concern due to the human body constantly extracting nutrients from the air.

Basements are an issue due to most toxins being heavier than air and they will accumulate in the lowest area of the home. You should avoid spending extended time in basements as they generally have the most toxic air in the home. If you do spend extended time in a basement, then you should ensure that there is a source of fresh air coming into the area.

For those of you with indoor cats, you should be changing out the cat litter regularly. Keep the cat litter at the furthest point from the bedrooms and get into the habit of checking it several times per day.

Make sure that your kitchen trash can seals in the smells and empty it daily. Keep it near to an outdoor air vent.

It is important to pay attention to the smells in your home and I do recommend the installation of an upper and lower air vent in every home to facilitate an exchange of outdoor air into the home. If you are breathing stale air due to lack of ventilation, then you may start to get sick.

"The flower that smells the sweetest is shy and lowly."

William Wordsworth

Temperature

The optimal temperature for the human body appears to be around 70 to 80 degrees Fahrenheit. It is interesting to note that the temperature of the forest floor in the tropics is a stable 72 degrees Fahrenheit. Research for this book is indicating that this is the correct human environment for excellent health.

If you go below 70 degrees Fahrenheit, you will get cold and start to shiver if you do not put clothing on. Above 80 degrees Fahrenheit you will start to get hot and fatigued.

Humans have developed heating and cooling systems to enable them to live anywhere that they want to. Exposure to these systems is likely to have health implications by cycling your temperature up and down, between indoor and outdoor environments. It is better to live in a location that is in harmony with your body and does not require artificial systems to keep you comfortable.

Two story homes should be avoided with heating and cooling systems. They typically end up with a hot upstairs and a cool downstairs. It is impossible to get an even temperature throughout the home. Single story homes do not exhibit this problem.

When you look into the native people in the Southwest USA, you notice that they were nomadic. They would live in the mountains where it was cooler in summertime and relocate to the lower elevations in wintertime where it was warmer. Nature provides the correct human environments all year round, you just have to follow them!

Plants are the same. Seeds only germinate in a narrow range of temperatures. If the temperature changes and is outside of this range then germination will not occur. As you can see, temperature is very important in plants too!

As the temperatures change around the globe in response to climate change, we will see a great change in the range and species of all life around the world. There is a possibility that it will eradicate humanity if the shift in temperature is too large in either direction.

People have long associated health conditions with changes in temperature. Arthritis is well known for people to report pains when the weather goes cold. Many arthritis sufferers develop an uncanny ability to predict the weather!

"Even if temperatures and conditions went flat from this point forward, we anticipate that Arctic ice would eventually disappear."

Ted Scambos

Humidity

Humidity is very important in human health and it is the amount of water vapor in the air. Too much or too little can be undesirable. The ideal level of humidity appears to be about 35% to 50% for excellent human health.

Low humidity typically occurs in winter when you heat your home. The heat reduces the humidity levels. Low humidity can bring:

- Sore throats.
- Sinus pains.
- Dry skin.
- Chapped lips.
- Itchy eyes.
- Excessive thirst.
- Static discharges.

You can bring up the humidity levels in your home by using a humidifier. Too much humidity can bring:

- Sweating problems.
- Breathing problems.
- Condensation.
- Dust mites.
- Mold.
- Mildew.
- Fungus.

- Spores.

- Musty smells.

- Wood will expand and windows and doors may stick.

    Everything will have a damp feel to it. It is a good reason not to buy homes that are frequently in clouds or fog. If humidity levels get too high in the home, then you can bring them down by using a dehumidifier.

"Know how weather, especially humidity, can affect the movement of doors and windows."

Marilyn vos Savant

Light

You would think that after thousands of years of studying the Sun, we would know everything there is to know about light but this is not the case. Light is only just starting to be understood in the human environment.

The many types of light appear to be able to induce the symptoms of Electromagnetic Hypersensitivity (EHS) into the human mind and body. Light is part of the electromagnetic spectrum and it should come as no surprise that it is able to induce similar problems that other types of radiation can produce in the human body.

One of the things that had me a little confused when researching this section of the book was the symptoms of Electromagnetic Hypersensitivity (EHS) occurring without the presence of electrical and electronic equipment. I later realized that there is no place on Earth that is free of man-made electromagnetic radiation with the advent of ground based radio and microwave transmissions and later, Space satellites that are routinely beaming electromagnetic energy to the surface of the Earth.

The types of man-made electromagnetic radiation are shown on the next page.

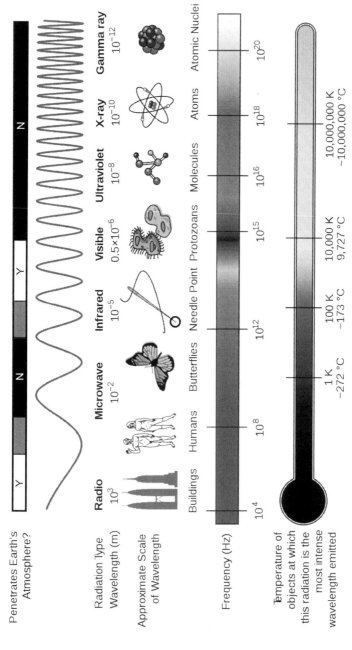

This makes it somewhat difficult to research the natural human solar radiation environment, as it is no longer natural! When outside, you are now subjected to a wide range of man-made electromagnetic frequencies that were not there just a few years ago. The man-made electromagnetic spectrum is increasing on a daily basis as the human addiction to modern technologies continues to gain momentum.

At the same time as the use of technology is increasing, we are witnessing the rise of human illness, cancer and the shortening of the human lifespan. They are all connected and it would be foolish to ignore this fact. Indeed, in 2011 the link between cancer and cellphones has become established. Cellphones in the future may be viewed the same way that asbestos and cigarettes are today.

Aside from the soup of man-made electromagnetic radiation that we now find ourselves immersed into, we have changed the atmospheric gas composition drastically over the last few hundred years of the Industrial Revolution. This is commonly referred to by many as the carbon levels rising in the atmosphere. They are approximately at double the levels recorded in the historical records and there are no doubts that the use of fossil fuels to drive the Industrial Revolution caused this to occur.

So why is this a problem for solar radiation? Well, it is not just the levels of carbon that went up, it is the levels of almost everything else that went up too! There is far more water vapor stored in the atmosphere from the over use of modern crop farming techniques that use irrigation, and this is just one of the many examples of things that have changed the atmospheric gasses. The problem with far more molecules in the atmosphere is that they will do a number of things:

- Block the Sun's rays.
- Heat up.
- Start moving more energetically.

- Create solar radiation interference effects.

- Interference effects may lead to illness, disease, cancer and premature death in humans, and throughout the natural world.

But it does not stop there. The addition of certain chemicals to the atmosphere will destroy wavelengths of light and it may only be a matter of time before one of these wavelengths of light that is critical for human survival is eliminated. This is called:

The Extinction Wavelength

The extinction wavelength of light may be achieved in the near future that could lead to the mass extinction of the human race. So, for sunlight and human health, atmospheric pollution is an extremely serious problem! It is entirely possible that we may achieve the extinction wavelength within the next fifty years and that will mark the start of the end for humanity.

Looking at the diagram on the next page, we can see that the atmosphere is already removing parts of the solar radiation spectrum at sea level. This wavelength reduction effect is at its worst in polluted cities, especially ones nearer to the poles.

With each passing year the solar radiation spectrum is slowly changing. As the atmosphere fills up with molecules from pollution we will move towards increasing filtering and interference effects from the Sun. Increased sunlight filtering and interference is likely to increase the disease rates in all living organisms, including the human.

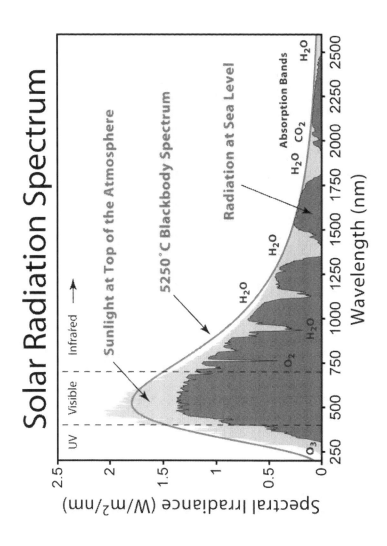

We can see this effect in plants. Plant leaves change with different solar radiation levels. The same plant will change the color, shape and size of the leaves to match the level of solar radiation that it receives. There is a limit to how adaptable each plant is and if the radiation gets outside of its range, the plant will start to show stress and may die.

Photosynthesis also occurs in the human body when it is exposed to sunlight. The latest research is indicating that the photosynthesis effects that take place within the human mind and body are extensive and wide ranging, and that vitamin D production is just one small part of it. Light has major functions in:

- **Modulating heart rate.**
- **Circadian rhythms.**
- **Digestion.**
- **Hormones.**
- **Mood.**
- **Fear.**
- **Mental state.**
- **Blood.**
- **Skin.**
- **Bone development.**
- **Mental development.**

Some of the ports of entry of natural light into the human body are:

- **Skin.**
- **Ears.**
- **Eyes.**

- **Nose.**
- **Lips.**
- **Nails.**

Painting nails is a human habit that may cause damage to the human body by covering up the blood that is circulating in the nail bed. Using lipstick may have the same effect on the blood circulating in the lips. It will prevent this blood from being irradiated by the Sun.

Is the wet surface of the eye providing regulation to the blood plasma? Irradiation of the saline solution of the eye may be essential to the proper functioning of the blood plasma.

Hair creates interference effects that modify the sunlight to an interference form of light. Dr. John Nash Ott noted that when he started to spend the majority of his time outdoors that his thinning hair started to regrow! Indeed, the hair regrowth industry markets ultraviolet and infrared light treatments as hair regrowth products. You do not need to purchase these products, as nature provides the treatments for free! Simply by spending time outdoors in the shade of trees should stimulate the hair regrowth effect.

The human mind and body may need to receive sunlight through the tree canopy in order to be in a healthy state. I call this light "Interference Green Light" and it may be the top thing that you need to be receiving in order to be in good health and free of pain. It is very different from direct sunlight due to:

- A much lower power level.
- It is filtered.
- It has interference.

Unfortunately in modern society, there are a large number of people who are sunlight deficient. This occurs through the use of cars, homes, offices, indoor shopping, and so on. The importance of getting daily Sun exposure has been lost on the modern generation and it is making them ill in large numbers.

Daily irradiation of the human mind and body by natural sunlight is an extremely important aspect of human health.

So how much sunlight should you aim for every day in order to be healthy? It is unique to each person. Typically a person with light skin needs less time and a person with dark skin needs more time outdoors. You should aim to spend as much of your day as possible outside in a natural environment, preferably in the shade of the tree canopy.

Toxic light presents a hazard to human health. There are many sources of toxic light and you should learn to recognize these sources. Potentially toxic light is almost everywhere in modern society:

- Artificial street lighting.
- Artificial home lighting.
- Artificial office lighting.
- Anywhere where there is glass.
- In your car.
- In your home.
- In your office.
- Televisions of every type.
- Computer monitors of every type.
- At sunrise.
- At sunset.
- Near the north and south poles.
- In any large city.

- In chemical trails from aircraft.

- In polluted atmosphere.

- Anywhere where the tree canopy is not present.

So what may toxic light be shown to do in the future? In the future the following conditions may be proven to be related to toxic light:

- Developmental problems.

- Cancer.

- Depression.

- Heart attacks.

- Circulation issues.

- Diabetes.

- Brain and nerve issues.

- Disruption of circadian rhythm.

- General aches and pains.

- Aggression.

- Psychiatric problems.

- Many of the current medical problems in society may be related to toxic light.

Humans tend to develop their land with modern agriculture and construction techniques which are not conducive to the natural world. It is ironic that through this unnatural development of their land that modern humans actually create environments that are unhealthy for them. Humans who develop their land in unnatural ways, such as clearing, introducing modern farming techniques, paving with concrete, and building tall structures really should not be surprised if their health deteriorates and they die prematurely.

Light sources come in many forms and here is a list in the order of quality of light:

- Under the tree canopy:
  - The best form of light for the human mind and body.
- Direct sunlight:
  - You need to be careful of this form of light as it is very powerful and may burn you. You can damage your eyes in this environment.
- Behind glass:
  - Glass filters light and removes wavelengths of light. Many types of glass excessively filter light to create a toxic form of light to the human mind and body.
- City sunlight:
  - The cities have many tall buildings that raise the radiation levels around them. The solar radiation levels in cities can be very high, have modified spectrums, and are extremely unpredictable.
- Artificial light:
  - Artificial lighting is not full spectrum daylight and may cause illness in the human mind and body.
- Office lighting:
  - This tends to be florescent lighting and is produced by just a few colors of wavelengths of light. It has a very spiked spectrum which does not occur in nature. The electronics that control them may emit electromagnetic interference (EMI).
- TV and computer monitors:
  - These tend to produce their colors from red, green and blue light and it is a very unusual spectrum

which does not occur in nature. The light is similar to florescent lights. The electronics that control them may emit electromagnetic interference (EMI).

- Street lights:

  ○ Street lights are predominantly gas discharge lighting and this is one of the most toxic forms of lighting to the human mind and body. The light tends to be monochromatic and they have problems with emitting electromagnetic interference (EMI).

- Neon signs:

  ○ These tend to have similar problems as streetlights.

You should be careful when choosing a home to live in and pay close attention to the location of streetlights. Streetlights can emit large amounts of electromagnetic interference, especially so when they switch on and also when they start to fail. The light also tends to be monochromatic and this type of light was shown by Dr. John Nash Ott to be harmful to biological systems. Indeed, I have noticed a trend in people who have died prematurely young and the presence of streetlights outside of their properties. The toxicity of streetlights has increased now that wireless transmitters are being installed into them.

The next diagram demonstrates the toxic effects of street lights. Electromagnetic interference (EMI), earth stray voltage, and stray currents will be looked into later in the book.

The following picture shows city nighttime light pollution in action. This area in San Diego is like daytime!

Streetlight Electromagnetic Interference

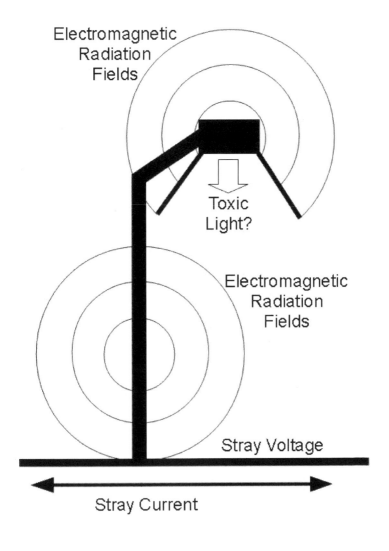

City Streetlights

This is a picture of nighttime in San Diego, California. The light pollution is evident and may be harmful to human health in the long term.

If you look at the next picture, it shows an effect that the tree canopy makes when solar radiation passes through it. This effect is called "Tree Canopy Light Interference". Light interference is a very big area of research in the optical and astronomical communities currently, it just has never been applied to the tree canopy.

Light is made up from waves and these waves can interfere with each other when passed through multiple apertures. The tree canopy makes many apertures that create the light interference effect. The result of this is that the solar radiation under the tree canopy is very different from the solar radiation above it. It is as different as night is to day.

The same effect occurs in water. The ripples on the surface of the water distort the light and create reflected interference light above the water and lensed interference light below the surface.

The interference wave diagram on the following page shows how the effect occurs.

Airy Disk Diffraction by Trees

The trees appear to produce the "Circle of Life" through tree canopy light interference.

Light Interference Diagram

The light waves arrive in parallel and expand outwards when they pass through the two apertures. Interference is produced where the waves intersect. This is seen as the bright and dark bands on the right. The dark is destructive and the bright is constructive interference.

For more information on interference:
http://electron9.phys.utk.edu/optics421/modules/m5/Interference.htm

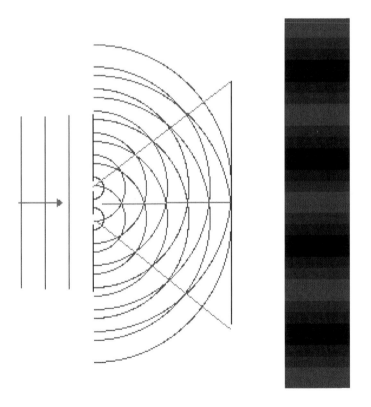

Interference of solar radiation may be caused by sunspots. Dr. Maki Takota showed that the presence of sunspots was related to the formation of certain chemicals in the blood. He also was able to relate blood chemistry to eclipses, solar flares, and sunrises.

A.L. Tchijevsky, a Russian professor, found a correlation between sunspot activity and human behavior. He linked major world events to the cycles of the sunspots! Generally, unrest was linked to sunspot maximum.

Sunspot minimum was linked to the occurrence of diseases in society by Professor d'Arsonval and others. It is not just human disease, crop production is affected too! Crops have a lower yield generally in sunspot minimum periods.

We really should not be surprised that sunspots can create changes in the human mind and body, as we have lived in the presence of the Sun for many thousands of years.

Sunspots do not cause much of a variance in solar irradiance levels from the Sun, typically oscillating up and down by just 1 watt per meter squared. It does not sound like much, but over the surface of the Earth, it is a huge amount of energy! The sunspot cycle is approximately eleven years and has been extensively studied by astronomers.

The picture on the next page shows the sunspot cycle and how the power levels vary.

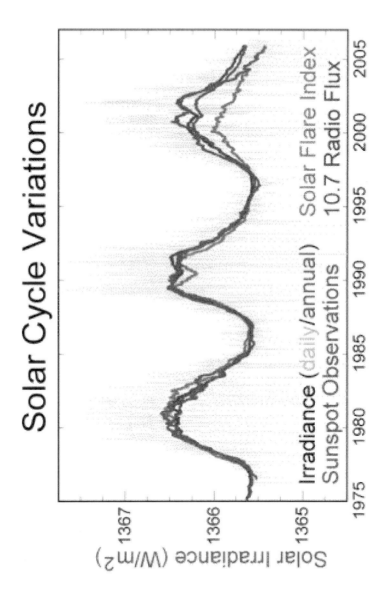

Unfortunately, it appears that little attention was paid to the sunspot effect during the development of the Space industry. We now have an Earth that has thousands of man-made satellites circling it. Every time one of these passes in front of the Sun, it creates a man-made Sun spot! The effects of this are currently unknown on the human mind and body.

Aircraft create a similar effect when they pass in front of the Sun. Unfortunately, they also leave a chemical trail behind them that may linger for hours. The chemical trail will act as a filter to the sunlight and may also create interference effects.

The diagram on the next page shows satellite or airplane interference effects on the Sun. The following photograph shows the effects of aircraft chemical trails on the Sun.

Satellite Interference

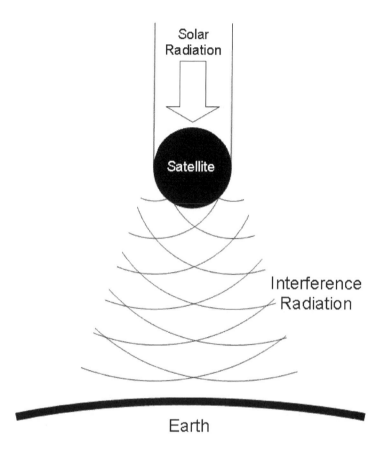

Aircraft Chemical Trails

The Sun as viewed entering an aircraft chemical trail. Many groups have shown up around the world, protesting the contamination of the sky and the strange optical effects that are clearly visible. Many people who live in such areas now relate their health problems to these effects.

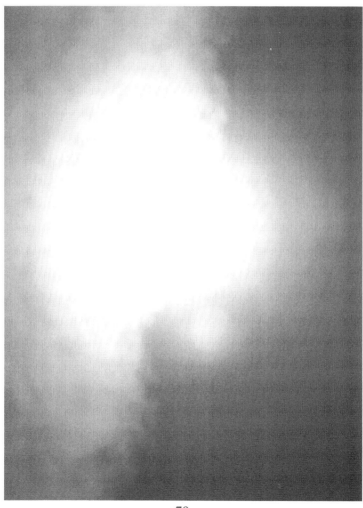

Dr. Abraham Hoffer was able to link the human mental state to sunlight and, in particular, the equinoxes and solstices. He found that mental functioning peaks in January and July, and normalizes after March and September.

Trees absorb the majority of the solar radiation and only reflect a small percentage of it back into the environment. They also change the color temperature and spectrum of the solar radiation. To sum up, here are the effects that the tree canopy has on solar radiation:

- **Interference of solar radiation.**
- **Significant reduction in the power level of solar radiation.**
- **Create a stable power level of solar radiation.**
- **Color temperature modification of solar radiation.**
- **Spectrum modification of solar radiation.**
- **Conversion of solar radiation into natural energy.**

Without the tree canopy reducing and modifying the solar radiation, humans are subjected to flicker. This is an effect that is happening at sub-second speeds that is not noticed by the human eye. However, a high speed camera that shoots several frames per second can see this occurring. The Sun is basically increasing and decreasing its intensity due to atmospheric distortions and interference. Astronomers know this effect as "Astronomical Seeing". This effect may be able to induce dizziness, fatigue, headaches, epilepsy and nausea. Modern flicker may be a consequence of atmospheric pollution and may be far more severe than in the past.

An effect that is similar to this is broken clouds passing in front of the Sun. These produce extreme power cycles in the solar radiation levels. The power levels can change by over 90% very quickly. The human mind and body appears to have problems with this high level of

frequent power cycling and again may experience dizziness, fatigue, headaches, epilepsy and nausea.

Solar radiation is made up of direct, diffuse and albedo radiation power levels. Direct is the view of the Sun's disk, diffuse is the sky in general (the blue and cloudy part) and albedo is the reflections. Of these, direct contains over 90% of the energy, diffuse contains under 10%, and there is no limit on the power level that the albedo can be at. In a modern environment, such as a city, the reflections can increase the power levels many times higher than the sky based solar radiation of direct and diffuse combined.

Dr. John Nash Ott found that increasing the ultraviolet energy content of light can cause cells to rupture. You need to be careful in areas of unnaturally high ultraviolet radiation due to the effects that it may have on the human mind and body. The peak areas in society for these ultraviolet effects appears to occur around glass covered buildings. When around such buildings, you should wear a hat, cover up, and pass through the areas of high ultraviolet radiation quickly.

In areas around tall glass covered buildings, the sky is very different. If you look up at certain times of the day, you may actually see two or more Sun's in the sky! You will see the real Sun and one or more reflected Sun's. This increases the ground based radiation levels and the effect on human health is not fully understood yet. Until it is, it pays to exercise caution around it. The effect is called "The Multiple-Sun Effect".

This effect was headline news in 2010 and the press called it the "Las Vegas Death Ray" due to a curved, mirrored, glass covered hotel in Las Vegas exhibiting the problem. The radiation levels on the ground were getting so high that the plastic drinking cups were melting! One can only wonder what extended exposure to the human mind and body would cause. The effect of focusing sunlight with mirrors was documented by Archimedes a long time ago as the "Archimedes Death Ray" and its purpose was for setting invading ships on fire.

The following pages show some of the solar radiation effects that you should be aware of:

The "Multiple-Sun" Effect

Building glass can create the "Multiple-Sun" effect.

The "Multiple-Shadow" Effect

The "Multiple-Shadow" effect accompanies the "Multiple-Sun" effect. The bright area on the right is higher in solar radiation power than Space!

"Archimedes Death Ray" Effect

Curved buildings can create the "Archimedes Death Ray".

"Multiple-Sun" Effect in Cars

The "Multiple-Sun" effect occurs in cars.

Possible Interference Cloud Formation

Holes in the clouds may cause filtering, interference effects, and high solar radiation cycling on the human mind and body.

Colors in Clouds

Colors in clouds may be solar radiation interference effects.

So you are worried about artificial lighting and are thinking that you can fix it by using full spectrum lighting products? Think again! While full spectrum lighting products sound appealing, the truth is that there is no such thing as full spectrum artificial lighting. It is a marketing ploy.

What full spectrum really means is that the light is as close to the Sun's spectrum as can be possibly made using current technology. Unfortunately, it is not sunlight and never will be.

All types of artificial lighting have the possibility of making you ill. Artificial lighting should be avoided if your health is important to you.

If you are going to have artificial lighting in your environment, then it should have a plant in front of it so that the light becomes modified by the plant. This is shown on the next page.

Light Modification by Plants

Here is the "Star of Bethlehem" as produced by a halogen lamp and a plant.

Color temperatures can be used to specify light sources. Here is a list of the color temperatures in Kelvin of modern light sources, as listed on Wikipedia:

- 1,700K Match flame.
- 1,850K Candle flame, sunset/sunrise.
- 2,700–3,300K Incandescent light bulb.
- 3,350K Studio "CP" light.
- 3,400K Studio lamps, photofloods, etc.
- 4,100K Moonlight, xenon arc lamp.
- 5,000K Horizon daylight.
- 5,500–6,000K Vertical daylight, electronic flash.
- 6,500K Daylight, overcast.
- 9,300K CRT screen.

As can be seen, the color temperature varies between the different sources and also the different times of the day.

The Color Rendering Index, or CRI for short, is similar to the color temperature. Wikipedia says the *"Color rendering index, or CRI, is a measure of the quality of color light, devised by the International Commission on Illumination (CIE). It generally ranges from zero for a source like a low-pressure sodium vapor lamp, which is monochromatic, to one hundred, for a source like an incandescent light bulb, which emits essentially blackbody radiation. It is related to color temperature, in that the CRI measures for a pair of light sources can only be compared if they have the same color temperature. A standard "cool white" fluorescent lamp will have a CRI near 62."*

The color temperature and CRI do not give the full picture. You also need to be aware of the radiation spectrum. Unfortunately, most gas discharge lamps have a spiked radiation spectrum that does not occur in nature. Due to this, you should avoid any artificial lighting that is created from gas discharge sources, such as mercury vapor, fluorescent, sodium, neon, and so on.

Dr. John Nash Ott found that he could change the gender of plants and animals simply by changing the color temperature of the artificial lights that they were exposed to! A very interesting effect of artificial lighting and it is a good reason to ensure that you have the correct lighting products in your home and office, and particularly around babies and developing children.

Mercury based lighting mystifies me. We know that mercury is toxic to humans. So why would we make lighting products with it? Dr. John Nash Ott extensively demonstrated in his books that many mercury lighting products appear to be harmful to human health.

The next page shows how the florescent (mercury) and tungsten (traditional) light bulb spectrums compare.

Florescent Spectrum

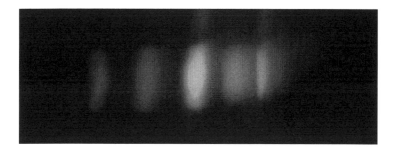

Note that the spectral lines are not continuous, but rather broken up. This is typical of gas discharge lighting. It does not occur in nature.

Tungsten Spectrum

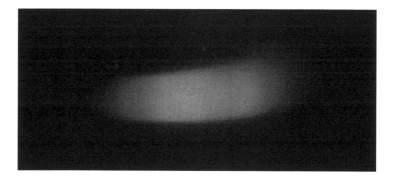

A smooth continuous spectrum that is typical of what nature produces.

I would recommend that you avoid the use of the new lighting that has been developed, such as gas discharge and light emitting diode (LED) lighting. These have been developed in order to use less energy at the expense of the quality of the light. They are typically not comparable to natural sources of light and they may make you ill in the long term.

All artificial lighting should be generated by heat. This is how the Sun generates light. Unfortunately, there are no man-made sources of lighting that can generate the same temperature as the Sun. Halogen filament lighting is about as close as it gets.

Television and computer displays of all types are sources of artificial light. You should be wary of your exposure to these as they may be able to impact your health.

The recent adoption of large screen televisions may bring with it an increase in human health problems in the future. People watching three dimensional images frequently may be an issue in the long term. Both of these could possibly be like a ticking time bomb. It is recommended that if you have a display in your environment that you keep it as small as possible. You may want to experiment with the brightness and contrast controls to get it to emit the lowest amount of light and still be comfortable to use. It is advised that your screen should not dominate your field of view.

Use your display in an environment that has good lighting in it and plenty of plants. Your display should not be the brightest thing in your environment.

So what is a healthy level of lighting? If we take a look at the forest environment, then the answer is obvious. Keep daytime lighting levels equivalent to outdoor shade values and use plants in front of artificial lights to create light filtering and interference. Use natural plants in front of your windows to create light filtering and interference. If indoors, you should sit facing the window during the daytime so that your eyes can sense the changing levels of daylight. It is preferable for your windows to be at eye level when seated so that you can see the outdoors through them.

A simple way of gauging the indoor daytime light environment for the human is to do a light test. Turn off your indoor lighting in the middle of the day. Note how bright the surroundings are. Now turn on your indoor lights and see if it is brighter. If the indoor environment is brighter then it means that you need to have more natural light coming in to your daytime areas. You can do this by adding more windows or skylights.

You should be aiming to illuminate your indoor daytime environment with natural outdoor light, not electrical lighting products. This light should be full spectrum natural light that the intensity can be controlled with window shades. Working in daytime environments that are illuminated with artificial lighting products is undesirable for human health.

If you work in a daytime indoor environment, then the lighting should mimic what nature does. It should have a natural daytime spectrum of light that matches outdoor daylight. This would be achieved with full spectrum filament lights that have the correct amount of blue and ultraviolet light in their spectrums to mimic outdoor daylight. Your indoor lighting level should be approximately 1,000 lux (Lux is a measurement of brightness of light).

From 10:00 to 14:00 there should be an additional set of lights that is turned on that increases the brightness of the office environment, to mimic the peak in daylight that occurs outdoors. The indoor environment during this time should have an illumination level of approximately 2,000 lux. You can easily achieve this in your office environment by simply having a desk lamp that you switch on during that time to increase the light illumination that you are exposed to. You should be using full spectrum filament light bulbs of the correct spectral emissions for this exposure.

You should make sure that you go outdoors for an hour at solar noon and sit in the shade of trees. Do not wear any sunglasses, glasses, contacts, make-up, nor sunscreen for this exposure. You need this exposure daily to keep up the solar cycle in the human mind and body. Without it, you may start to get fatigued as the day goes on. Daily outdoor exposure to sunlight is very important if you have an indoor occupation.

If you do not get the correct light exposures in the day, then your sleep cycle may kick in. The human mind and body when kept in an indoor environment of low lux light will not realize that it is daytime, as it cannot sense the increasing levels of daylight that the genetics are accustomed to. As such, by late morning your body may start sending a signal for you to sleep!

If you can, during any of your daily breaks, you should try and go outdoors to get natural daylight. You will also be getting fresh air and pollen exposure, which are also necessary for good health.

The recommended cycle for indoor daytime lighting is shown on the next page.

Indoor Daytime Lighting Cycle for Human Health

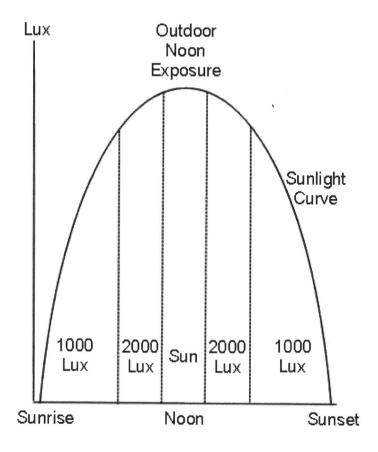

Nighttime lighting is very different from daytime lighting. You want to be using products that have minimal blue light in them. Blue light exposure is well known to cause insomnia. If you install lighting products that have too much blue light in their spectrums, then you may enter into a life of insomnia and not realize that it is your light bulbs that are causing it! Insomnia rapidly leads to fatigue and onto depression. These daytime lighting products are commonly sold as "Daylight" or "Full Spectrum" light bulbs and should not be used in nighttime applications.

You should stick to the tried and tested filament light bulbs for your nighttime exposures. Avoid the compact florescent and LED bulbs as some of these are well known for their excessive blue light content. Keep your lights low, as bright light can also trigger insomnia.

Most people do not actually realize it, but they are polluting the interior of their homes with nighttime electric lighting. This pollution has become quite severe in the last few decades with the adoption of compact florescent lights (CFL) and light emitting diode (LED) products. These products typically have unnatural spectrums of light and can have a wide range of electromagnetic interference emissions from them. Some of them give out too much blue light and this may induce insomnia and macular degeneration of the eye. They can turn the home wiring into a radio transmitter which may lead to Electromagnetic Hypersensitivity in the human.

I currently advise people to use filament bulbs. I presently use conventional filament light bulbs for nighttime lighting at my home. I keep the lighting low and just sufficient for what I am doing.

Low voltage halogen lighting products should be avoided due to the emissions from them. They may have high amounts of man-made ultraviolet light, some create dirty electricity, and electric and magnetic fields. Man-made ultraviolet light is known for its ability to cause skin and eye problems and ultraviolet light is not present during the nighttime in nature. You will not find any electronic lamp dimmers in my home, as they are a product that you should avoid using. Lamp dimmers can create dirty electricity, electric and magnetic fields.

You should also be using the correct voltage light bulb. In the USA these are sold as either 120 volt or 130 volt light bulbs. You should be using the 120 volt versions, as they are far more efficient at producing light. The 130 volt versions should only be used if your light bulbs are frequently breaking within a few days of installing them. If you use 130 volt light bulbs when they are not needed, your light bulbs will last a very long time, but will give out a poor quality of light.

You should be aware that the many sources of artificial lighting can affect your mental and physical health. You should be choosing your daytime artificial lighting products based on the proven health benefits of "Full Spectrum" light bulbs that are comparable to outdoor daylight. Health benefits have been reported by many gardeners who use these products to grow their plants indoors during the winter months. Nighttime artificial lighting products are different to daytime products and should be used in your home for good sleep patterns.

Nighttime over-illumination is a problem in the modern world and it may be able to affect your health. Keep it as low as possible during the nighttime and only increase lighting levels if you feel that you need more light in your environment. You should think candles, not necessarily use candles, but rather the illumination level that candles create. There is a reason why candles are considered romantic and it is likely related to the low level of light that they create.

If you have your environment too bright during the nighttime, then you may upset the circadian rhythm that governs your sleep cycles. Keep lighting as low as possible during the nighttime. You should also keep your skin covered as much as possible to prevent it from absorbing the artificial light.

You should be wary of computer monitors and televisions, as their light can be very unnatural and may induce a wide range of health problems into you. The most common problem is insomnia and this can be reduced by adjusting the blue color on the monitor lower and minimal brightness. Using televisions and computers after dark is not advisable and may adversely affect your sleep.

During the daytime, you should use your computer next to a shady full spectrum window to dilute the artificial light from the monitor with natural daylight. If you work in an office where you cannot see the outdoors, then you should place a full spectrum diffused light behind your monitor with plants to give you a more natural light exposure to the eyes and skin.

The correct daytime alignment of a computer monitor is shown in the next picture.

It is likely that daytime office environments would be healthier if the ceiling was painted sky blue and the walls had green nature landscape scenes on them. Clearly, the office staff sitting facing shady full spectrum windows is already proven for its beneficial health effects and has been so for many decades. You should be aiming to keep your environment as natural as possible for good human health. Natural potted plants can assist in this process in the office environment.

A spectrograph can be used to assess the quality of light in your environment and you can buy affordable spectrographs from scientific education suppliers and astronomical shops. You can easily build a simple spectrograph out of a cardboard box and a compact disk to enable you to assess the different types of lighting products in your environment. I built mine in just ten minutes! This is shown on the following pages.

Computer Screen Alignment

The correct alignment of a computer screen to the shaded full spectrum ultraviolet transmitting acrylic window. You should try and ensure that you have a natural view behind a computer monitor during the daytime.

Spectrograph Design

Here is the design of a cereal box spectrograph using a standard compact disk, from:
http://www.cs.cmu.edu/~zhuxj/astro/html/spectrometer.html

Spectrograph

Here is the cereal box spectrograph.

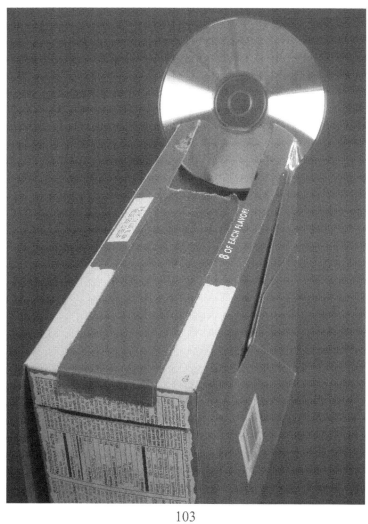

Spectrograph in Operation

A spectrum of a florescent light produced by the cereal box spectrograph. Note the bands of distinct colors of light. These do not occur in light produced by nature.

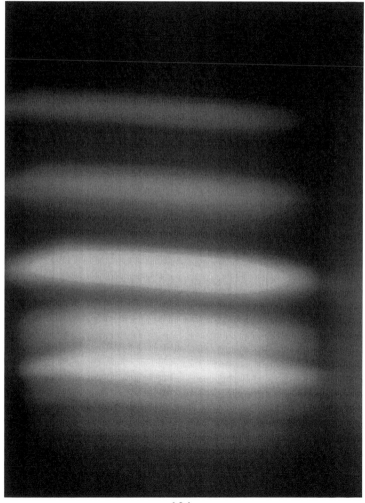

Incorrect radiation levels may be able to affect your sex drive and it may be proven in the future that human sex drive is governed more by radiation types and levels than any other factor, even more so than hormones! Generally, a feeling of contentment replaces sexual desire in natural radiation environments.

We are constantly walking around in an energy field of broad spectrum solar radiation that originated at the largest nuclear reactor in the solar system, called the Sun. It is important that this energy level be kept low for human health. The trees and plants, also known as nature, provide this function and aid human health.

You should avoid watching the sunrises and sunsets regularly due to the filtered nature of the solar radiation. It is this filtering that generates the amazing colors. Unfortunately, staring at the Sun during this time appears to be bad for human health. It may have the potential to make you ill through solar radiation induced disease if it becomes a regular habit. You should be wary of the orange and red colors that occur during this time, as they may be a product of atmospheric pollution.

General exposure to the direct view of the Sun delivers a lot of energy to your mind and body and this can be felt as heat and also sensed by the eyes as brightness and you may need to wear sunglasses due to this. There are no doubts that the Sun is a carcinogen in the wrong situation and it is wise to avoid direct views of it in a developed environment.

Glass rooms, such as conservatories, should be avoided. They are generally full of reflections and these boost the radiation levels inside them. If you have one of these rooms, you would be wise to fill it with plant life in order to reduce the solar radiation levels inside it.

East, equatorial (south in northern hemisphere and north in southern hemisphere) and west facing windows let in a lot of direct solar radiation. You should not spend time too close to windows in this orientation. Window shades and coverings are recommended. Plants should be placed next to windows like this. Desks should not be placed under

windows that have direct sunlight as you will get overheated and fatigued. Longer term, you may develop radiation sickness.

As for your eyes, ultraviolet (UV) blocking sunglasses should be worn when the solar radiation levels are unnaturally high and these should be of an appropriate level of neutral density optical material. Mirrored, colored or polarized lenses should be avoided due to the modification of the solar radiation that takes place with these. Solar and artificial radiation viewed through glasses and contact lenses may be able to impact your health and you should only wear them as needed. You should view the light that your eyes receive as a nutrient and you want to keep it as natural as possible.

A picture of the Sun through a pair of tri-focal glasses is shown on the next page. Bi-focal and tri-focal glasses may be a particular issue for solar radiation transmission to the eye.

Sunlight Through Tri-focal Glasses

The Sun appears to have magnification, filtering, and interference effects when viewed through tri-focal glasses.

Anything unnatural that filters the broad spectrum of solar radiation will create an artificial and possibly toxic environment for humans. Unnaturally filtering sunlight may cause it to create electromagnetic interference (EMI) effects in the human body. We will discuss the effects of EMI later.

Glass coatings modify the solar radiation spectrum on both the outside and inside of the glass. Many of these coatings cannot be seen by the human eye and the glass will appear to be transparent to optical light. The glass may be highly reflective to other wavelengths such as ultraviolet (UV), infrared (IR), microwave, radio, and so on.

The following pictures show the difference between outdoor light and indoor light. The first picture was taken outside looking at the reflection of the metal plate on the bench. The second picture was taken from inside the home looking through a coated double glazed window and mesh screen. As can be seen, the white outdoor light changes to yellow with many rainbow colored spikes when viewed from inside the home.

Outside Light

The reflected white sunlight from the bench, as photographed outdoors. Note the wisps of light.

Inside Light

This picture was taken from inside the home through coated double glazed glass and a mesh screen. Note the yellow light and the rainbow effects in the spikes.

The atmosphere when mixed with pollution is just like a window coating. If you fill the atmosphere with toxins, then you really cannot be surprised if the solar radiation transmission through it becomes toxic to humans.

The next picture shows the Sun as viewed from the window of an airplane. As you can see, the Sun is white, but the reflection from the ocean is orange! The filtering of the sunlight by the polluted atmosphere has changed the color of the sunlight to orange.

The following picture shows the pollution that can be found hanging over Los Angeles, California. This will filter the sunlight during the day and the astronomical light during the night. It is not a good idea to live in large cities such as this if your health is important to you.

The Sun as Viewed from an Airplane.

This picture was taken from an airplane window at cruising altitude in the Pacific ocean near to Hawaii. Note the white Sun and orange reflection below.

City Pollution

The band of atmospheric pollution hanging over Los Angeles, California, as viewed from the Griffith Observatory. Pollution will unnaturally filter light.

This appears to be the current understanding of solar radiation power levels on the human mind and body:

Too Low: Sunlight deficiency, developmental problems, deformities in babies, bone deformity in the young, rickets, system deficiencies, low vitamin D, low vitamin B12, high cholesterol, muscle weakness, legs may feel heavy, difficulty moving, aches and pains, hunger, vomiting, nausea, diarrhea, obesity, anxiety, stress, mental issues, fatigue, depression symptoms, headaches, moodiness, eye issues, Attention Deficit Disorder (ADD), Autism, general illness, shorter or longer life span (reduced aging effects from sunlight exposure may lengthen the lifespan, whereas the sickness effects of the deficiencies may shorten it).

Low: Extended lifespan from reduced solar radiation aging effects.

Normal: Unlimited energy during the day. Good sleep patterns. Excellent health. Clear thinking. Normal development. Normal life span.

Above Normal: Extended life span from increased radiation exposure, system under stress, general illness.

High: Accelerated development, may have reduced height as an adult, accelerated aging, going gray prematurely, hypochondriac symptoms, sleep problems, anxiety, stress, eye issues, mental issues, fatigue, depression, random aches and pains, itchy skin, hot skin, system overload, immune system compromised, cold sores, intestinal problems.

Too High: In addition to above: Deformities in babies, bone deformity in the young, frequent illness, onset of disease, most likely premature death.

Extreme: In addition to above: Rapid onset of disease, major eye issues, premature death.

Unnatural sources of radiation (such as mercury lamps) may change the speed of progression of these problems and will most likely speed it up.

Constantly changing between the different levels (high cycling) may be able to induce mental instability or depression.

Changing from low solar radiation exposure to high during a day may cause an intoxication effect to occur. You may feel hungover the next day if you are sunlight deficient.

It is well known that life expectancy is modified according to radiation exposure. The next graph shows what I have been able to ascertain about how this occurs.

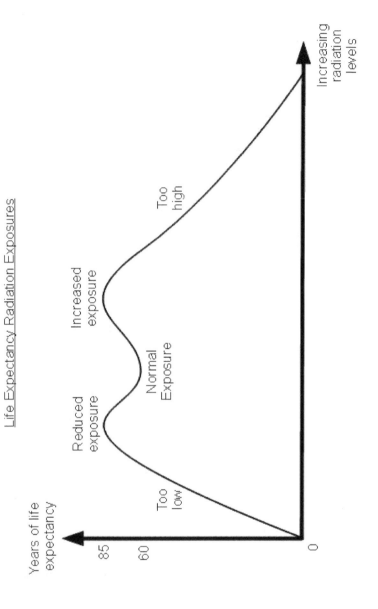

The definition of a normal level of solar radiation for humans is a forested environment in the tropics that has a tree canopy. This is due to the "Tree Canopy Light Interference" effect.

The human skin is referred to by many as the largest organ of the human body. As the largest organ, it also has the largest task in the body. It is your suit of armor against the environment and for it to work well requires attention on your part.

The human skin is sensitive to radiation. Expose it to solar radiation and it will start to react to it and make changes to the human mind and body. The levels of radiation of all types needs to be controlled to natural levels in order for the changes that they create to be beneficial to humans.

The use of sunscreens are not recommended. Sunscreens act like window coatings and modify the solar radiation received by the body. There is much talk about sunscreen being potentially poisonous to the human body. Instead, use natural methods such as shade, an umbrella, a wide brimmed hat, and white clothing to protect yourself from excessive Sun exposure. It is interesting to note that human clothing styles changed significantly over the last century and prior to this it was normal to cover up the human body when in sunlight. Exposing lots of skin to the direct view of the Sun is a relatively new trend in humans, as is sunbathing.

Many traditional cultures have understood the need to cover up the skin when in direct sunlight and, in men, to grow beards. Keeping hair to its natural length in all parts of the body appears to be a protector against radiation. Of interest is that hair may do this through the use of solar radiation interference as well as blocking the radiation.

If your eyes or body get too much Sun exposure and start to exhibit problem(s), you should retreat indoors and allow the problem(s) to clear up. You should still get daily outdoor exposure, but stay in the shade and keep it to about an hour until you fully recover. You will need to be careful that you do not go into sunlight withdrawal when recovering from Sun damage.

The human mind and body has a very advanced photosynthesis mechanism that keeps it functioning well. It is important that the human mind and body is exposed daily to the natural light that occurs in nature and this is found under the tree canopy in a green natural environment. The UK has found this out the hard way with 20% of the children tested showing signs of rickets in 2010!

Clear ultra-violet (UV) transmitting acrylic window products are available and are commonly used by zoo's to prevent the animals becoming vitamin D deficient. It is recommended that you have these products installed where you spend the bulk of your daytime activities. This is especially important around developing children, as UV is known to be important in the correct development of children. Products that are specifically marketed for this purpose are "Monkey Shine" Solarcryl SUVT and LuciteLux Utran UVT. These are products that are commonly used in tanning beds and they have a high UV light transmission. You can easily obtain these products from tanning bed manufacturers and suppliers.

I have installed this in my office and my kitchen where I spend most of my day. My initial findings are that it has helped improve the final health problem that I am trying to eliminate, which is occasional fatigue. If you have developing babies and children, then you should install this in areas where they spend the bulk of their daytime. Full spectrum windows are particularly important for them. You do not need to install this in areas where you spend your evening and nighttime, such as bedrooms and bathrooms.

You should be aware that you can get sunburned through these products and that many things, such as plastics, may suffer from ultraviolet degradation. It is preferable to install UV transmitting glazing in areas that are shaded, such as the side of your home that faces the pole. In sunny locations, you should ensure that your window shades and coverings can sufficiently reduce the sunlight levels to prevent you from getting sunburn!

Dr. John Nash Ott installed UV transmitting plastic windows in his home. This was due to noticing that his plants were not growing correctly indoors behind the glass windows. The UV transmitting products that he used improved the growth patterns. He also said that it improved his own health. He reported having better eyesight, thicker hair, far fewer incidences of colds and the flu, and excellent health after installing it.

There is one last thing that we need to look into and that is the question of "What is nighttime?". One answer to this question that I have heard is that it is an absence of daylight. Having given it some thought and become aware of effects that are taking place in plants during the nighttime, I now know this not to be entirely correct.

Nighttime appears to be a heavily filtered and interference form of daytime. There is some daylight still present during the night, it is just that our human eyes are not able to detect it. Animals that have night vision have evolved with eyes that are able to function in this much lower level of daylight. Illumination by the stars becomes prevalent, each of which is a nuclear reactor. The cycles of the moon and planets come into play, as do comets and shooting stars. Nighttime also has a very different radio frequency environment due to the lack of ionization of the atmosphere from solar radiation absorption.

On the way to nighttime we pass through the period known as sunset. This period marks a distinct change that lasts approximately two hours where great changes in the lighting levels and types of radiation occur. At sunset as the Sun is coming down to the horizon, the light becomes an interference type of light due to crossing the horizon and also by being heavily filtered by the atmosphere. The same effect happens at sunrise. Sunrise is different from sunset due to the air being cooler. As such, less interference and filtering effects take place during sunrise.

The diagram on the next page shows the cycles of light over one day. The following diagram shows the solar radiation daytime and nighttime effects that take place. The last diagram shows the interference effects that may occur during a solar eclipse by the Moon.

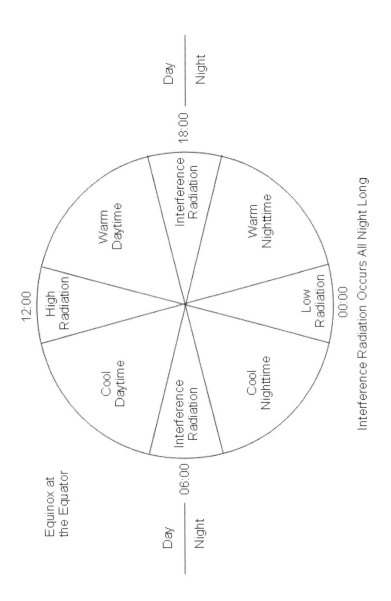

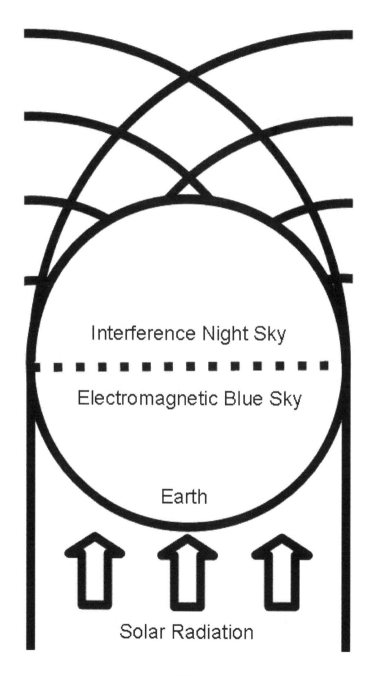

Moon Interference with Earth

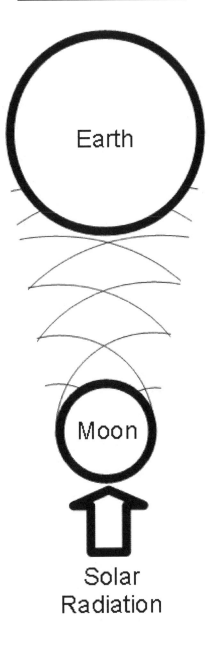

Light in the human environment is an extensive subject that has many more facets than what we can cover in this chapter. As such, more information on light in the human environment can be found in my book on the subject, called "Toxic Light".

"Health and Light" by Dr. John Nash Ott is also recommended for further reading on this subject.

The human health advantages of effective Sun exposure are documented in the following books:

- "Sunlight" by Zane R. Kime MD MS.
- "The Healing Sun: Sunlight and Health in the 21st Century" by Richard Hobday PhD.
- "Light: Medicine of the Future" by Jacob Liberman OD PhD.
- "The UV Advantage" by Michael F Holick PhD MD and Mark Jenkins.

Trees are extensively documented for their health and healing powers on the human mind and body and the following books are recommended reading:

- "The Healing Power of Forests: The Philosophy Behind Restoring Earth's Balance with Native Trees." by Akira Miyawaki and Elgene O. Box.
- "The Healing Power of Trees: Spiritual Journeys Through the Celtic Calendar." by Sharlyn Hidalgo.

"Eating the Sun: How Plants Power the Planet" by Oliver Martin explores the solar functions of plants further.

"Only a full spectrum of natural light could promote full health in plants, animals, and humans."

Dr. John Nash Ott

Sleep

One of the things that has disappeared for many people is their quality of sleep. I can associate with this as I was plagued with insomnia for many years that I eventually traced to side effects of medications, artificial lighting products and electromagnetic interference exposures. How wonderful it was to get great sleep patterns back!

Most biological damage appears to occur during sleep. Sleep is the regeneration process of the mind and body and for it to work well requires the natural environmental conditions that humans evolved in.

You should pay close attention to your bedroom environment. You should be concerned when you open your eyes in the middle of the night and can see things. Your bedroom should be completely dark while you sleep. You should not be able to see anything!

Things that should not be in your bedroom are:

- Night lights.
- LED clocks.
- Cell phones.
- Wireless products.
- Electricity.
- Products that glow.

Your bedroom is where you go to biologically regenerate. It must be completely dark for this process to work well. It is undesirable to have electricity in the room and electrical products as they may interfere with the regeneration process. If you have light coming into the room, then you should purchase blackout blinds to prevent it. You should regard your bedroom as a refuge of darkness where you recharge for the next day of light. Simply Yin and Yang.

One of the techniques that I developed when recovering my health was rotational sleeping. I developed this technique when I became aware that there are now biological hotspots of wireless radiation in homes today. The technique revolves around making sure that you do not sleep in the same position each night. The simplest form of the technique is to move your pillow to the opposite end of the bed from the previous night, so that you rotate 180 degrees each night. I prefer to sleep in a four position rotation cycle and this works well in large beds. I follow this pattern in a large bed:

1. **Left side of bed.**
2. **Rotate 180 degrees.**
3. **Right side of bed.**
4. **Rotate 180 degrees.**

This means that if there is a biological hotspot where your head rests, then it will only be subjected to that hotspot one night in every four. You should pay attention to how you feel when you wake up each day and if one of the positions is constantly making you fatigued in the morning, you should consider moving your bed to a different location.

A useful technique for assessing the quality of the environment in your bedrooms is the "Goldilocks" test. If you have multiple bedrooms, then spend a week sleeping in each bedroom and see how you feel. The bedroom that you wake up feeling really refreshed in is the one where you should sleep.

If there is a high powered transmitter near to your home, then you should align your bed so that it presents the least bodily area to the transmitter. It is preferable to have your feet pointing toward the transmitter and your head pointing away from it.

This configuration will ensure the least irradiation of the brain occurs, as it will be shielded by the body.

If you are raising babies and children, I recommend that you sleep in their rooms for a week and see how you feel. If you are not waking up refreshed, then it is likely that they are not waking up refreshed either. If this is the case, you should consider moving them into another room or have an expert come in to assess what the problem is in the bedroom. I recommend that parents of Autistic children change the bedroom that their Autistic child sleeps in to see if it improves their health.

Sleeping on the floor is known for its health benefits and many people do it. The radio frequency fields are very low at the ground and I have found that it improved my health for several months after being subjected to a high powered pulsed radio frequency field from the utility meter. You should make sure that the floor that you are sleeping on does not have stray voltage or any electrical cables running through it. I eventually had to stop sleeping on my floor due to seasonal stray voltage/current/frequency detrimental health effects that showed up as the voltage on the floor increased. I suspect that this sleeping on the floor technique may be beneficial to some Autistic children.

Metal bed frames with metal mattresses are undesirable in a wireless radiation society. The metal coil mattress is an antenna system that will have a wide range of electromagnetic energy flowing on it. Metal can be radioactive if it was contaminated during its manufacture. Occasionally, an X-ray machine will be melted down during the metal recycling process and contaminate the entire batch of metal. Metal also disturbs the natural magnetic field of the Earth and this is undesirable for the cellular regeneration processes. Melanoma and breast cancer are suspected to be linked to sleeping on metal coil mattresses.

Wooden bed frames with natural foam mattresses are recommended. A low wooden bed frame that keeps you about one foot above the floor appears to be the ideal height to avoid stray voltage/current/frequency exposures that may be on the concrete floor and for reducing exposure to radio frequencies. If you have electrical wiring running under the wooden floor that your bed is on, then it is recommended to have the fields of that wiring assessed and to ensure that the mattress is high enough off the floor to avoid those fields. Keep the bed out of the electrical wiring fields that may be in the walls by keeping it a few feet away from the wall or by turning off the bedroom electrical circuit during the night.

Nature defines the human sleep environment as dark with low radiation levels and you should ensure that during the nighttime that you are sleeping in this environment.

"In order for the light to shine so brightly, the darkness must be present."

Francis Bacon

Radiation

"It is clear that radiation produces the electrical current which operates adaptively the organism as a whole, producing memory, reason, imagination, emotion, the special senses, secretions, muscular action, the response to infection, normal growth, and the growth of benign tumors and cancers, all of which are governed adaptively by the electric charges that are generated by the short wave or ionizing radiation in protoplasm."

Dr. George Crile

Most people associate radiation with nuclear bombs, nuclear power plants and X-ray machines. This is a very blinkered view and we will show you how extensive radiation in the human environment is and how critical it is for human health.

The modern human has created a radiation environment that has never existed before in all of human history and it keeps on adding to it every year. This is an issue as most of the sources of man-made radiation are not yet fully understood. As a radiation society, we are running before we have even learned to crawl!

The radiation environment started to significantly change at the start of the Industrial Revolution when the steam engines started to fill the atmosphere with water vapor, wood and coal burning emissions. This later progressed onto gas and oil burning in the late 1800's as the wood and coal became harder to source. How would this affect the radiation environment? Well, by cutting down the trees, the tree canopy was destroyed which caused the solar radiation levels to significantly increase!

The tree canopy typically reduces the solar radiation power levels between 10 and 30 times less through absorption and modification of the solar radiation. This is important to human health as the mind and body does not function well in a direct view of the Sun and may eventually get ill.

It is somewhat ironic that during the settling of the USA, that the government required many of the settlers to clear the land that was given to them! Poor health born out of greatly increased solar radiation levels may have followed this action.

As for the emissions into the atmosphere, this has changed the solar radiation transmission from Space to the ground. The solar radiation all around the world is now significantly different from what it was just a few hundred years ago. As the emissions continue into the atmosphere, the solar radiation will become changed so much that many people will start to become ill with radiation sickness. In some parts of the world, it is likely that this is already happening.

But solar radiation is just a small part of the story. The human radiation environment has many aspects to it:

- Solar radiation.

- Environmental radiation.

- Radio waves.

- Microwaves.

- Electrical and electronic radiation.

Environmental radiation can come from many sources:

- Cosmic radiation.

- Electrical storms.

- Replacing nature with modern development significantly raises the levels of many types of radiation.

- Mining activities bring radioactive minerals to the surface which will increase the background radiation levels.

- Fall out from nuclear bombs and power plant disasters.

- Living close to a nuclear power station.

- Living close to a power generation plant.

- Living at altitude.

- Living near large bodies of water.

- Living in snowy climates.

- Living close to a military base.

- Living close to an airport or port.

- Living close to any type of broadcast antenna.

- Living close to power poles and lines.

- Living close to tall structures.

Man-made electrical and electronic radiation did not exist until the 1700's when scientists started to discover the various forms of it. We have progressed extremely quickly from a new discovery to the many forms of it that are now present in modern society and this seems to have happened with little thought to the consequences to human health.

We now live in a society that is bombarded by electrical, electronic and wireless radiation. There is no place in the world that it does not reach with the prolific adoption of satellite and radio communications. Future historians will likely document this as one of the most foolish things that humanity ever did.

The electrical, electronic and wireless interference is commonly called:

- Electromagnetic Interference (EMI).

- Radio Frequency Interference (RFI).

- Microwave Frequency Interference (MFI).

For the purposes of this book we will use EMI to cover all of these effects. The health effects of electromagnetic interference are commonly found documented as:

- Electromagnetic Hypersensitivity (EHS).
- Electro-Hyper-Sensitivity (EHS).
- Electrical Sensitivity (ES).
- Electro-Sensitivity (ES).
- Radio Wave Sickness (RWS).
- Rapid Aging Syndrome (RAS).
- Electrical Poisoning.
- Electronic Poisoning.
- Wireless Poisoning.
- Radiation Poisoning.
- Radiation Sickness.

For the purpose of this book we will use the term Electromagnetic Hypersensitivity (EHS), as they are all essentially the same thing. The strange thing about EHS is that many people have it, but very few of them realize that it is EHS that is causing their problems. EHS has not been publicized well and even many doctors do not appear to be aware of it. Strange, considering the amount of electrical, electronic and wireless products that we are now exposed to.

EHS is somewhat of an "Inconvenient Truth" and if it became widely accepted that it was causing human health problems, then many things would have to change. Industry and governments do not like change and in order to avoid it, it is far easier to deny it. For this reason, you should be aware of your environment and of EHS so that you can stay safe until it does become widely acknowledged as being the problem that it is.

The symptoms of it can be:

- Neurological:
    - Headaches.
    - Dizziness.
    - Nausea.
    - Difficulty concentrating.
    - Memory loss.
    - Irritability.
    - Dementia.
    - Depression.
    - Anxiety.
    - Insomnia.
    - Fatigue.
    - Weakness.
    - Tremors.
    - Numbness.
    - Tingling.
    - Seizures.
    - Paralysis.
    - Psychosis.
    - Stroke.
- Cardiac:
    - Palpitations.
    - Arrhythmia.
    - Pain or pressure in the chest.
    - Low or high blood pressure.
    - Slow or fast heart rate.

- Respiratory:
  - Shortness of breath.
  - Sinusitis.
  - Bronchitis.
  - Pneumonia.
  - Asthma.
  - Flu-like symptoms.
  - Fever.
- Dermatological:
  - Skin rash.
  - Itching.
  - Burning.
  - Facial flushing.
- Opthalmological:
  - Pain or burning in the eyes.
  - Pressure in or behind the eyes.
  - Deteriorating vision.
  - Floaters.
  - Cataracts.
- Muscular & Skeletal:
  - Muscle spasms.
  - Altered reflexes.
  - Muscle and joint pain.
  - Leg or foot pain.
  - Arthritis.
  - Swollen joints.
  - Joint irritation.

- Others:
  - Sexual problems.
  - Digestive problems.
  - Abdominal pain.
  - Enlarged thyroid.
  - Testicular or ovarian pain.
  - Dryness of lips, tongue, mouth or eyes.
  - Great thirst.
  - Dehydration.
  - Nose bleeds.
  - Internal bleeding.
  - Altered sugar metabolism.
  - Immune abnormalities.
  - Redistribution of metals within the body.
  - Hair loss.
  - Pain in the teeth.
  - Deteriorating fillings.
  - Impaired sense of smell.
  - Ringing in the ears.

Exposure to high frequencies may cause:

- Irregular heartbeat.
- Pains.
- Allergies.
- Miscarriages.
- Birth defects.

- Childhood leukemia.

- Brain tumors.

- Reproductive tumors.

- Cancers.

- Infertility.

- Depression.

- Chronic Fatigue Syndrome (CFS).

- Fibromyalgia.

- Gulf War Syndrome.

- Alzhiemer's disease.

- Parkinson's disease.

- Lou Gehrig's disease.

- Behcet's disease.

- Sexual arousal.

- Aggression.

- Hearing things. (Loud bangs, high pitched buzzing, low frequency hum)

- Smell of smoke when there is no smoke.

Dr. Jim Burch PhD of the Cancer Prevention and Control Program at the University of South Carolina, has documented the biological effects of radio frequencies on the human mind and body as:

- **Cell proliferation (Increased ODC activity).**

- **Ion flux across biological membranes (Ca^{++}).**

- **DNA damage (Comet assay is an example).**

- **Gene expression (Oncogenes, stress proteins).**

- **Altered enzyme activity (Radical pairs).**
- **Immune system perturbations.**
- **Endocrine disruption (Melatonin for example).**
- **Altered blood-brain barrier.**
- **Autonomic nerve function (EEG, ECG).**
- **Sleep or circadian rhythm disruption.**
- **Headaches, neurological effects.**
- **Reproduction disorders.**
- **Carcinogenesis (Brain, leukemia).**

EMI can be classed as narrow-band or wide-band:

Narrow-band EMI sources can be:

- Smart meters/smart devices/automatic meter readers (AMR)/advanced metering infrastructure (AMI) utility wireless networks.
- Two way radios (transceivers).
- Cordless phones, mobile phones and cell phones.
- Wireless scanners and wireless checkout devices.
- Radio frequency identification devices (RFID).
- Wi-Fi networking.
- Television and radio transmission towers.
- Cell phone towers.
- RADAR systems.
- Rural internet and satellite internet.

Here are some sources of wide-band EMI:

- Computers.
- Cathode ray tube (CRT) TV's.
- Digital flat screen TV's.
- Power lines.
- Electric switches and relays.
- Electric motors.
- Variable frequency drives.
- Thermostats.
- Bug zappers.
- Inverter systems.
- Florescent lights.
- Compact florescent lights (CFL).
- Light emitting diode (LED) lights.
- Neon signs.
- Stereo systems.
- MP3 players.
- Electronic lamp dimmer switches.
- Cars.
- Transportation systems.
- Electric and electronic toys.
- Battery powered watches.

Most digital equipment will have broadband emissions from it. If it is switching a large amount of power, then it may produce large amounts of electromagnetic interference.

There was a shift that occurred largely in the 1980's from analogue electronics to digital electronics. Analogue

electronics did not have a digital microprocessor chip in it and was made out of many basic electrical and electronic components. More importantly, it did not have the high speed pulsing that characterizes digital electronics. It is this high speed pulsing that causes digital electronics to be generally very high electromagnetic interference producing equipment.

The pictures on the following pages show the effects of electromagnetic interference on the human body voltage.

The Human Body Voltage

The human body voltage appears like a capacitor charging and discharging when in contact with conductive flooring that is electrically grounded with stray voltage.

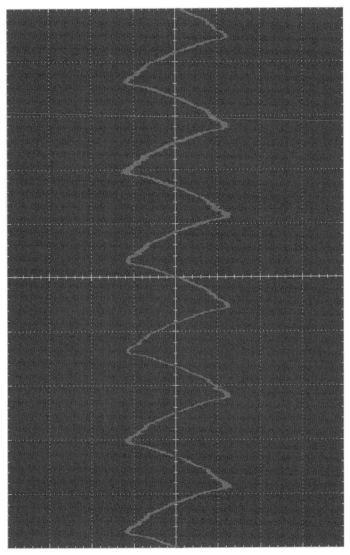

The Human Body Frequency Spectrum

A Fast Fourier Transform (FFT) reveals the many frequencies contained within the human body. Zero Hertz is at the bottom and the high frequencies are at the top.

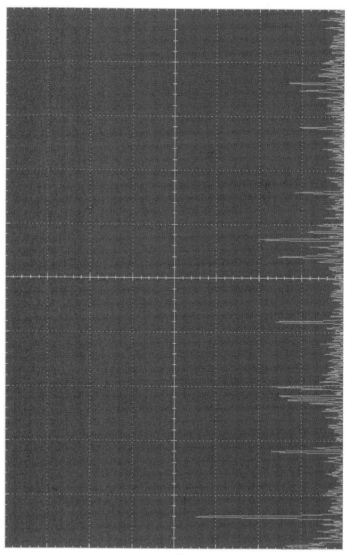

Digital electronics uses electrical square waves to drive it. A square wave is one of the dirtiest electrical waves and as such it has many harmonics associated with it. Harmonics are the many different frequencies of sine waves that must be added together to produce the square wave. Basically, if you have a 60 Hertz square wave, then it will contain many higher frequencies of sine waves to produce it. They may be thousands of times higher in frequency than the wave that they are part of. It is for this reason that a standard AM radio when tuned into static can detect electrical noise. It is the harmonics that it is detecting in the square wave.

Computers function on high speed switching of square waves. For this reason you will find some very interesting microwave, radio, electric and magnetic fields around them. The fields vary with the age of the computer and the different brands of computers. Laptop computers can be a particular problem due to the electronics being located below the keyboard and mouse pad. Some of these areas underneath can have very high levels of EMI producing electronics! It is best with a laptop computer to switch to a large font on the display, push the laptop back and use a separate keyboard and mouse to control it. You should avoid putting it on your lap.

Compact florescent lights appear to produce radio waves from their power switching electronics. These radio emissions appear to vary between the different sizes of bulbs and also how old they are. It is not a good idea to bring radio frequency producing equipment into your environment and for this reason I advise people against using these products. Testing has shown that these products can couple their electromagnetic fields into water and cause stray voltage effects. This is a concern due to the human body being between 70% to 90% water, depending on age. Light emitting diode (LED) bulbs appear to exhibit similar effects.

Florescent tanning booths and beds may be an electromagnetic interference hot zone and should probably be avoided. The tanning light spectrum may be an issue as well.

Some of the new digital televisions (TV) appear to be producing levels of electromagnetic interference that are affecting peoples health. I measured electromagnetic interference that was produced by my digital TV at a distance of fifty feet away from it! The electromagnetic interference that this particular 32" LCD flat screen TV was producing appeared to be of an interference type of radiation. There were pockets of low and high interference AM radio frequencies throughout the home. I had noticed plant deformity and leaf tip problems in the plants in the room of the digital TV which may be linked to the electromagnetic interference. The interesting thing about discontinuing the use of my digital TV was that plants started to grow in my garden that had appeared dormant for years! Plasma TV's appear to be the worst offenders of the new digital TV's with large electromagnetic interference fields around some of them.

It has been noticed that intensive care patients are leaving the hospital with brain problems that were not there prior to their treatment. It is likely to be an effect of electromagnetic interference exposure. Around an intensive care bed you will typically find many electronic displays that are all emitting EMI. Many hospitals now use wireless networking and there may be numerous wireless devices all transmitting very close to the patients brain. Long term exposure to EMI is known to do strange things to the brain including brain fog, headaches, fuzzy thinking, and memory loss. Indeed, the most wireless devices that I have ever seen in one place was in the maternity ward of Tucson Medical Center! The worst example of a really poor wireless device location was placing a wireless network router directly over the new born baby's cot!!!

Solar photovoltaic (PV) power systems on the roofs of residential homes may be an issue. The inverter system that converts the direct current electricity from them into alternating current appears to cause electromagnetic fields to occur on the equipment. The large scale adoption of solar photovoltaic systems in the home has not yet been around long enough to fully understand the health risks that they may present.

Due to the advent of digital equipment, the electrical circuits of the home may need to have line terminators installed in them. Line terminators prevent digital reflections from occurring on the home wiring. Essentially, it is an electrical noise reduction technique that can be used to help prevent the home wiring from emitting radio waves.

The radial electrical circuit is shown on the next page. The last socket may now need a line terminator installing into it to terminate the circuit to prevent electronic noise reflections from occurring. A line terminator is generally a small capacitor in parallel with a high impedance bleed resistor. This would be connected across the live and neutral terminals of the final socket in the radial circuit.

Terminating Radial Circuits

Radial electrical circuits may need line terminators installing at the last outlet.

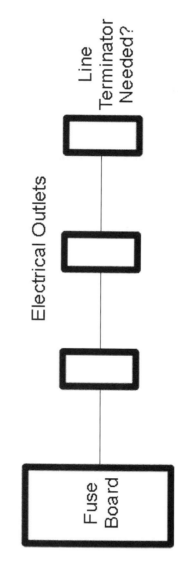

Line terminators prevent frequency reflections from occurring on the circuit. A line terminator is generally a capacitor and a resistor.

Cars and transportation systems can have high amounts of EMI associated with them. In the past this came from their ignition systems and could be heard on the car radio as a buzzing sound that would increase in line with the revolutions per minute (RPM) of the car engine. Today, there is likely to be more electromagnetic interference from the electronic systems of the car and this may include:

- Radio frequency identification devices (RFID).
- Hybrid drive system.
- Electric drive system.
- Engine computer system.
- Global Positioning Systems (GPS).
- Alternating current inverter system.
- Entertainment systems.
- Cell phone charger.
- Cell phone.

Using your cell phone in the car is a bad idea due to the radiation reflections that may occur. This may raise the radiation environment in the car and may cause interference effects that may be harmful to human health. Not to mention the distraction effect that may lead to a collision!

Electromagnetic interference is occurring with motorbikes and appears to be much stronger due to the compactness of a motorbike. Many motorbikes have their electronic systems and battery mounted under the seat and this area may emit the most electromagnetic interference into the rider. More details on this can be found in the book "Motorcycle Cancer?" by Randall Dale Chipkar.

The move to hybrid and electric cars appears to be taking place with little concern to the electromagnetic interference environment inside the car. There are reports of people detecting electromagnetic interference fields within these cars that can far exceed the 2 milli-gauss magnetic fields that the International Agency for Research on Cancer (IARC) have set as their limit for constant magnetic field level for safe human health. Other people have noticed that their children appear fatigued on a long drive in a hybrid car as opposed to a normal car. Hybrids and electric cars appear to emit high electromagnetic interference during acceleration that may be around 100 milli-gauss and up to 30 milli-gauss when cruising. Constant fields of 2 milli-gauss and above should be avoided due to the elevated cancer risk.

It is well known that frequent travelers have a high obesity risk. Transportation systems of all types can produce high electromagnetic interference environments. Planes, buses, streetcars and trains may be filled with electromagnetic interference and it is added to by people using their electronic devices on them.

Electronic lamp dimmers are one of the biggest culprits for producing electromagnetic interference effects within the home. I was quite surprised to find that a large and extensive electromagnetic field that I was detecting throughout a home was coming from a lamp dimmer! You should avoid these products and use the three way filament light bulbs instead.

Microwave ovens can produce similar effects. I have detected radio, microwave, electric and magnetic fields around these and, as such, I no longer use one. They make cell phones look safe!

People have started to realize that computer Wi-Fi networks, cell phone networks, DECT cordless phones, and the like are all causing biological problems.

When reviewing the Popular Science article *"The Man Who Was Allergic to Radio Waves"* we find that Per Segerback *"noticed his first symptoms -- dizziness, nausea, headaches, burning sensations and red blotches on his skin -- in the late 1980s, a decade into his telecommunications research work. All but two of the 20 or so other members of his group reported similar symptoms, he says, although his were by far the most severe. His EHS worsened and now, he says, even radar from low-flying aircraft can set it off."*

Electromagnetic Hypersensitivity (EHS) has been extensively documented in plants and trees around these electromagnetic fields. The biological effect in plants and trees is not new, it was extensively researched and documented by Dr. John Nash Ott in the 1950's. Indeed, I have grown plants in electromagnetic fields that exhibited the growth defects that he documented.

This is shown on the next page. The three plants all looked the same when I bought them. They are all Dieffenbachia's (Dumb Cane) and they all looked like the bushy one on the left. The center plant changed its growth in a Wi-Fi and AC voltage field location. The right plant changed its growth in a radio wave field that was produced by a 32" LCD digital television and now has very small and glossy green leaves with no patterning, as shown in the following picture. As you can see, they look like completely different species of plants and I call them my "Frankenstein" plants!

Electromagnetic Interference Effects in Plants

Exposure to EMI can cause plant deformity and growth defects. The leafy Dieffenbachia plant on the left is how the spindly ones to the right used to look before EMI exposure.

Dieffenbachia Leaves

On the left is a normal fully grown Dieffenbachia leaf. On the right is a fully grown Dieffenbachia leaf from the plant in the EMI field produced by my 32" LCD TV.

The switched mode power supply (SMPS) has replaced the traditional heavy block transformer that products used to be supplied with. This is a concern, as the switched mode power supply creates far more dirty electricity effects than the traditional transformer power supply. Indeed, some switched mode power supplies can completely fill the home with electromagnetic interference! Switched mode power supplies are poorly tested, inadequately regulated and are unfortunately powering most of the electronic products that you are purchasing that you plug into electrical sockets. It is likely that they will become highly regulated by the government in the future and I recommend that you should avoid buying electronic products until that occurs.

Babies and children are the most sensitive to the effects of EMI and particular attention should be paid to their environments. In a home with children you should avoid:

- Ionizing smoke detectors.

- Wireless baby monitors.

- Electrical and electronic toys.

- Radio controlled and wireless toys.

- Train sets and car race tracks that may produce sparks.

- Battery operated wristwatches.

- Avoid placing the baby to sleep on a party wall with your neighbor as you will not know what EMI producing equipment is on the other side of that wall.

- Avoid placing the baby to sleep near an electrical outlet.

- Avoid having electrical cables running along the floor where the baby may crawl.

- Avoid letting a baby crawl on a floor that may have electrical cables running underneath it. (Upper story of a home).

- Avoid living in apartments, as these present the biggest electromagnetic interference risk from the neighbors around you. A detached house is far better.

- Avoid letting a baby crawl on any type of electrically conductive flooring, such as tile or concrete.

- Keep babies and children away from electrical, electronic and wireless equipment in general.

Power lines and poles running through the streets is a bad idea. They have a number of problems that may lead to illness:

- **Magnetic fields.**

- **Electric fields.**

- **Electrostatic fields.**

- **Electrostatic attraction.**

- **Radio wave emissions.**

- **Plasma emissions.**

- **Ion emissions.**

- **Nitrogen emissions.**

- **Ozone emissions.**

- **Reflection and interference of sunlight.**

- **Reflection and interference of radio and microwaves.**

- **AC electrification of the ground around them (stray voltage, stray current, stray frequency).**

The utility power lines have setbacks that apply to them and for 13,800 volt AC lines, this setback is typically thirty feet either side of them. Building of homes and offices in these setbacks is generally not allowed due to the high electromagnetic fields that are present within the setback. The larger the voltage, the larger the setbacks become. Power line set backs can be several hundred feet wide on the high voltage transmission systems.

Power line radio emissions may be erratic, occurring only at certain times of the day or during certain weather conditions. They are generally caused by the induction of electrical energy into the surrounding metalwork on the power pole that can cause sparks to jump between the metalwork. A failing or dirty insulator may have a similar effect. When a power line starts to emit radio waves, these radio waves may extend beyond the power line set back. The radio waves cannot be heard or felt and a standard AM radio tuned to static (no radio station) can generally be used to detect them. Exposure to these radio waves may lead to Electromagnetic Hypersensitivity (EHS).

While developing the power line section of this book, I spent three hours each night for two nights examining the power poles and power lines in the area of my home. I noticed the following conditions occurring over the following weeks:

- **Headaches.**

- **Insomnia.**

- **Fatigue.**

- **Sore throat.**

- **Irregular heartbeats.**

- **Intestinal pains.**

- **General poor health.**

- **Heightened sexual desire occurred in the first few days after testing was finished, it appeared to be a side effect of electromagnetic interference withdrawal.**

You should not spend time directly under power lines, as this will put you into what appears to be a plasma field. Plasma is the fourth state of matter and under the power lines is an invisible flow of energy between the lines and the ground.

The electrostatic field is what appears to light up florescent tubes that are held near to power lines. It is a strange sensation to walk into a high powered electrostatic field as it is this field that makes your hair start to react. Nikola Tesla was trying to develop wireless lighting products using this field. We are fortunate that he never achieved his dream, as he may have made many people sick with his wireless lighting system. Nikola Tesla did end up being regarded as "nutty" and exposure to the electrostatic field may have been one of the things that was affecting him.

During my research into power lines producing AM radio frequencies, I noticed the reflection effect. The cell phone tower microwave signals seem to be interacting with the power lines and may be producing pockets of AM radio frequencies that can be picked up on a standard AM radio tuned to static. If you were in one of these pockets for an extended time period, you may develop Electromagnetic Hypersensitivity.

The following pages demonstrate the various effects of power lines.

Power lines and poles can have many types of large fields around them. "Dirty electricity" effects may cause extensive radio wave fields.

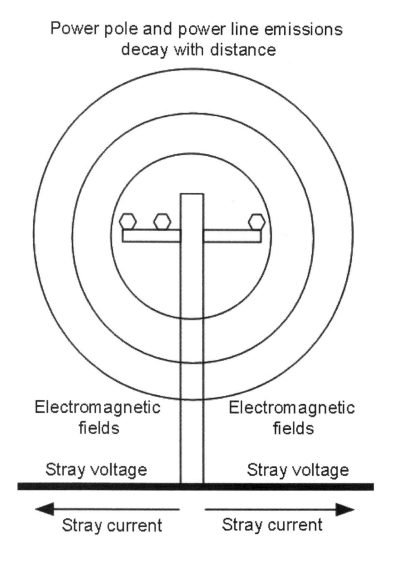

Power pole and power line emissions decay with distance

Electromagnetic fields

Electromagnetic fields

Stray voltage

Stray voltage

Stray current

Stray current

Power Pole Metal Work

Induction effects in power pole metal work may cause sparks to jump between it which will cause radio wave emissions to occur. Dirty and defective insulators do the same.

Power lines and poles can emit plasma and ions. The high voltage causes the electrostatic attraction effect. Power lines and poles have fields that extend out from the area that set backs should be applied to, to protect human health.

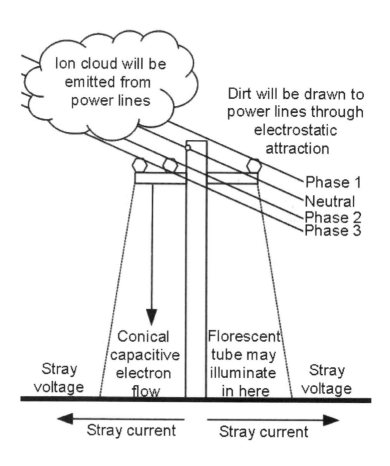

Power Line and Pole Solar Interference

The power poles and lines can interfere with the solar radiation transmission when in front of the Sun.

Power Line Reflections

Power lines may cause radio and microwave reflections and interference effects to occur.

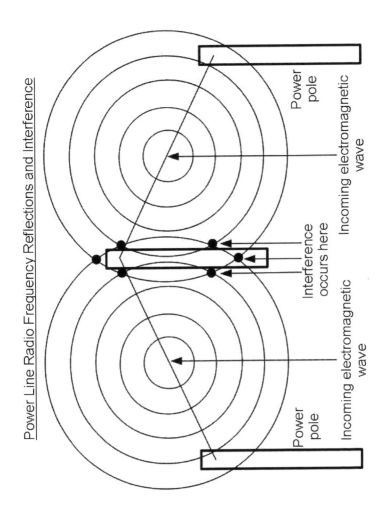

Power Line Radio Frequency Reflections and Interference

Dr. Phillip Stoddard, Professor of Biological Sciences at Florida International University, has done extensive research on utility power lines. He has found significant health risks from their presence:

- **The closer you live to a power line, the more likely you are to develop Leukemia.**
- **Living in a magnetic field of 3.5 milli-gauss doubles the Leukemia risk.**
- **Living within 0-50 meters of a power line doubles the risk of Alzhiemer's Disease and presents a 1.5 increased risk of developing Senile Dementia.**
- **Burying the power lines brings the magnetic fields closer.**

I do not recommend that you spend significant time underneath high voltage power lines, as you may be getting a free radiation treatment! They really should be fenced to keep people from venturing under them, especially young children. You should not buy a home that is underneath them if you value your health, as many people have become sick in such homes.

A common problem on buried power lines is the corrosion of the concentric neutral. The concentric neutral is the wire that you see wrapped around the outside of the utility cable that comes down the power pole. If this corrodes, then the neutral starts to become high impedance and this will cause current to increase though the ground. Basically, corrosion of the concentric neutral will electrify the surrounding ground and is clearly a human health hazard. Many people have been electrocuted by corroded neutrals after rains, due to the ground becoming more conductive to the stray electricity. Faulty insulation on the live conductor that causes leakage currents will have a similar effect.

It is not a good idea to live near to electrical equipment. The following locations should be avoided if you value your health:

- **Streetlights.**
- **Power lines.**
- **Power poles.**
- **Transformers.**
- **Substations.**
- **Switch yards.**
- **Power generation plants.**

The areas in the vicinity of these may have large amounts of stray voltages, stray frequencies and stray currents. This is shown in the next diagram.

Stray Voltage, Stray Current and Stray Frequency

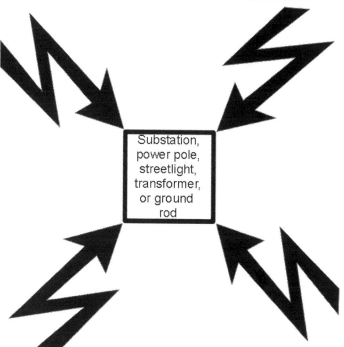

The earth around electrical equipment is commonly electrified by ground rods. You should avoid coming into contact with electrified earth, as it is a human health hazard. You should keep children away from these areas.

The electrical power system in your home may also affect your health. Around electrical fuse boards there may be very high microwave and radio fields, magnetic and electric fields, and stray voltage/current/frequencies. The electromagnetic interference is a function of:

- The quality of the utility power.
- The electrical equipment that is connected to the fuse board.
- Smart/AMR/AMI utility transmitting electrical meters.
- The type of structure that it is mounted to.
- The quality of the grounding system.
- The construction of the electrical fuse board.
- The routing of the cables that connect to the equipment.
- The presence of an alternate energy system (such as solar photovoltaics or wind turbines).

It may be possible that Leukemia in children is linked to the location of the fuse board on the home. The health of babies and children is a particular concern with the advent of Smart/AMR/AMI transmitting electrical utility meters, as they broadcast wireless radiation into their surrounding environment. Babies and children are the ones who are most affected by these effects.

Some fuse boards may need filters installing and line terminators on their radial circuits. These are important in areas that have electrical power quality issues (Dirty electricity).

The location considerations for electrical fuse boards and associated equipment is shown in the following two pictures.

Electrical Fuse Boards

These should not be mounted in human habitation areas due to the fields that extend out from them that may include wireless radio frequency transmitting fields. An ideal location is on the side of the garage.

Bad Fuse Board Location

Unfortunately, the fuse board in the previous picture was located directly behind the master bed! Electrical fuse boards should not be mounted on human habitations.

The utility supplies a combined ground (earth) and neutral connection to your home that splits into the ground (earth) and neutral connection at your fuse board. The ground rods that you may see near fuse boards are to effectively ground this combined ground (earth) and neutral cable to the ground potential of the property. The voltage on the ground (earth) and neutral connections will rise up and down in proportion to the load on the electrical system in your area if it is not grounded properly by both the utility and the homeowner.

You should remember that the electrical ground (earth) connection in your home or office connects directly to the neutral transformer winding connection that is supplying the electricity. It may be carrying an AC voltage!

This is shown in the diagram on the next page.

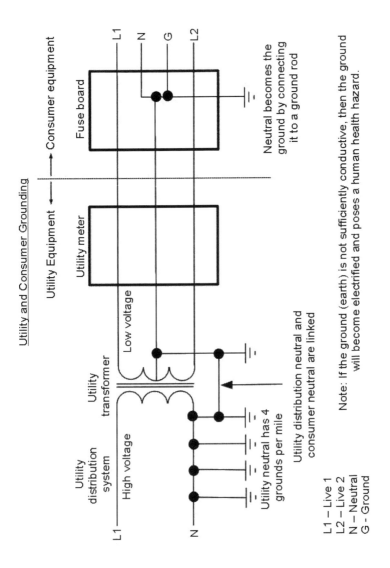

Utility and Consumer Grounding

L1 – Live 1
L2 – Live 2
N – Neutral
G - Ground

The concept of grounding is quite interesting. The electrical system was originally designed to be a one wire supply system with an earth return through grounding rods. It was only when people started to get shocked by the electrified earth that a return wire was also installed, which we now call the neutral. However, the ground rods remained and if the neutral is higher in voltage potential than the ground, then it will feed AC voltage and current into the ground. In other words, the ground rods electrify the ground with AC electricity! This is a particular problem anywhere where the ground is a poor conductor of electricity, such as the dry desert southwest USA.

You should be aware that anywhere that a ground rod is installed, that there may be AC voltage, frequency and current in the vicinity of it. The electrification of the earth may extend several hundred feet from the ground rods. You should keep your shoes on and keep children and pets away from these areas. AC electrification of the earth commonly occurs around fuse boards, streetlights, pad mounted transformers, power poles and lines, and electrical substations too! People who walk their dogs are at particular risk from these energized earth effects.

A utility electrical substation diagram is shown on the next page. The substation relies on an earth (ground) return path for the electricity and as such, the area around electrical substations may have large amounts of stray voltage, stray currents and stray frequencies present.

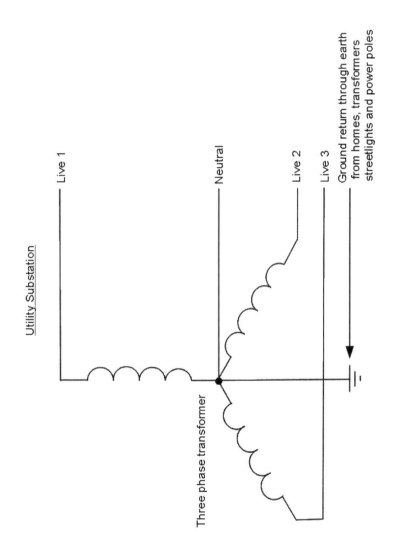

Grounding electrical systems at the home can create voltages in the home that are commonly referred to as "stray voltage". Stray voltage is a well known effect in the diary industry and it can wreak havoc on the health of farmers, their families, and their livestock. As one farmer reports *"It's a slow, painful tortuous death, is what it is for them,"* said Siewert, who with his father, Harlan, owns Siewert Holsteins in Zumbro Falls. *"It's like watching someone die of AIDS."*

One of the things that has caused stray voltage to become prevalent in the human environment is the widespread adoption of plastic services to homes. In the past, the plumbing was cast iron drains, galvanized steel supply pipes and copper tubing. All of these were relatively good conductors of electricity and supplied good grounding to the home. This has changed and plumbing is now commonly plastic, which is an insulator to electricity. Unfortunately, you may still find that the water in the plastic drains is electrified from the sewer in the street which in turn will electrify your toilets, showers, basins and baths. It is not a good idea to be urinating into an electrified toilet!

The stray voltage effects are shown on the following pages. The next picture shows the Amprobe 5XP-A multimeter logging the maximum voltage. The following diagram shows the stray voltage in my garden as measured in the evening at my home during September 2011 in Arizona, USA. As you can see, there is an AC voltage gradient from the ground rods at the front of the home to the back of the home where the reference ground rod is installed. The 8 foot long reference ground rod is installed well away from the home and electrical systems. There are no electrical connections to it.

Measuring Stray Voltage

The Amprobe 5XP-A multimeter is logging voltage values of the electrical outlet ground pin (Right probe) to the garden ground at the back of the home (Left probe).

Garden Stray Voltage

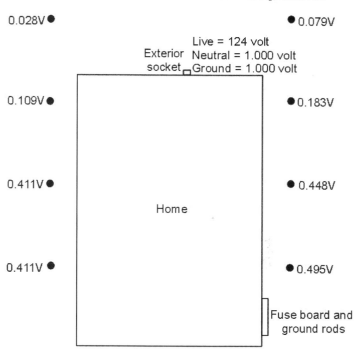

● 8 foot reference ground rod

0.028V ●   ● 0.079V

Live = 124 volt
Exterior Neutral = 1.000 volt
socket ⬜ Ground = 1.000 volt

0.109V ●   ● 0.183V

0.411V ●   ● 0.448V

Home

0.411V ●   ● 0.495V

Fuse board and
ground rods

Stray voltage measurements in the garden using an
Amprobe 5XP-A multimeter. As can be seen, there is a
voltage gradient through the property.

During logging both current and voltage with an Amprobe 5XP-A multimeter in August and September 2011, these are the range of values that I recorded at my home:

- 0.07 to 1.66 volts.
- 2.7 to 55 milli-amps.
- 60 Hertz AC.
- Low values occurred near sunrise, high values occurred between 16:00 to 20:00 mid-week.
- The electrical distribution network had high loads due to air conditioning loads running in the summer heat.

It is interesting to note that for electrocution to occur in water, the following conditions must exist:

- Assuming a wet human body resistance of 300 ohms.
- Muscle control in the human is lost at between 6 to 30 milli-amps.
- 1.8 to 9 volts of 60 Hertz AC is needed.

As we can see, the conditions at my home are very close to those required for a water electrocution. If a surge from an electrical fault or lightning strike on the utility system occurred, then the conditions for a water electrocution may occur. I would be very concerned if I owned a swimming pool!

Plastic plumbing may well be hazardous to human health, as it does not ground the water contained within the pipes. As such, any plastic plumbing that is routed with electrical cables may start to couple into the electrical field of the cables. The result is the water may become electrified. You may well end up with stray voltage at your faucets, basins, showers and bathtubs! Clearly an undesirable effect. The structuring of the water that may occur has unknown health effects.

Stray voltage in the past was commonly associated with swimming pools and hot tubs, but is now rapidly becoming prevalent in many other areas throughout modern society. Have you ever wondered why competent swimmers drown in their own swimming pools? It may well be stray current that killed them, particularly if an electrical fault or lightning strike occurred in the area. Electricity easily couples into water systems and electrifies the water.

Antistatic devices (ASD) are commonly used in many industries and may present a health hazard to those who work with these. If they are connected into a poor quality grounding system, then they may well cause an AC voltage to appear on the human body. My research into this area is indicating that direct, long term exposure to a low level AC voltage may cause the human body to slowly fall into illness and perhaps onto disease. It matches the findings of the diary industry that just 0.5 volt of AC electricity exposure can lead to illness in biological systems. The effects that I noticed during two weeks of wearing an antistatic wrist strap that was connected to the electrical grounding system were:

- **Headaches.**
- **Insomnia.**
- **Fatigue.**
- **Irregular heartbeats.**

It was easily cured by removing the antistatic wrist strap. The symptoms cleared up within a few weeks. When I investigated the grounding system I found 1.5 volts of AC electricity on it when compared to the garden non-electrified ground rod and a wide range of frequencies extending into the megahertz range!

Antistatic equipment is common in the hospital operating room. Dr. William Rae determined that his allergic and neurological symptoms were caused by the electromagnetic fields in the operating room. He subsequently discovered that he was not alone in his hypersensitivity, and that there was a growing population of patients with the same condition. These people are typically told by their physicians that their symptoms are "all in their minds" and that they should seek psychiatric care.

Whether you use an antistatic device or not, you may find yourself connected into the AC supply through your environment. Walking around in your bare feet or socks on conductive flooring, such as tile or outdoors, may expose you to an AC voltage. Believe it or not, walking the dog may expose you to AC voltage through the dog lead if it is conductive! Also using any device that has a metal case and is electrically grounded through the cable may expose you to an AC voltage. Metal sewing machines, metal mobile homes, metal appliances, metal electric power tools and metal kitchen equipment can be examples of this. Anything that is conductive and electrically grounded that humans come into contact with is a potential health risk. Keeping your shoes on can reduce the risk, as can wearing electrically insulated gloves.

Plants can be affected by stray voltage and they may show retarded or accelerated growth, deformed growth or go dormant. In extreme cases they may die.

Stray voltage varies with the time of the day and can change quickly. Early in the morning it can be very low and during the peak electrical load periods, it can be very high. A multimeter with a minimum and maximum logging feature is ideal to find the range of values of stray voltage. I have found the Amprobe 5XP-A multimeter to be ideal for this purpose, as it has a 16 day battery life when using a 9 volt alkaline battery.

Whether you like it or not, stray voltage, stray currents and stray frequencies are present within your own body. The body will couple into electrical fields and this can be detected with a digital multimeter or an oscilloscope. The alternating current (AC) voltage on the human body can get

quite high, often exceeding fifteen volts when next to an AC cable. Just 0.5 volt of stray AC voltage is known to affect animals and just 2 volts of AC voltage is known to kill them! The farming industry has set an upper limit on stray voltage of 0.5 volt due to the effects that have been observed in the animals.

The electrical grounding system on my home in August and September 2011 regularly exceeded this value by three times the allowable animal contact value! I have noticed sore knees and aching bones occurring every year at summertime in my current home which I now have linked to this stray voltage effect.

To establish the biological toxicity of my electrified conductive tiled flooring, I placed three Dieffenbachia plants with their soil and roots in contact with the flooring. These were placed in the master bathroom (least electrified), front hallway, and in the kitchen (most electrified). The master bathroom Dieffenbachia grew very well, far better growth than my control plants that are grown in the extensive radio frequency fields that are present throughout my home from transmitting utility meters and distant cell phone towers. This matches what many people who use the earthing health technique report. The growth pattern degraded closer to the street that I have established is electrified with stray voltage. The worst growth was the kitchen floor plant that was very close to the utility equipment and their transmitting utility meters. There are no doubts that electrified flooring is biologically harmful and you should avoid walking barefoot or sitting on such flooring.

The following picture shows the three plants used in the electrified flooring experiment.

Electrified Flooring Experiment

From left to right we can see the degrading growth patterns of the Dieffenbachia when the roots and soil are connected to electrified flooring. The left one with the best growth patterns was connected to the least electrified floor and the right plant with the most deformed and retarded growth was connected to the most electrified floor nearest to the utility equipment.

The characteristics that are observed in animals that have been exposed to stray voltage are:

- Reduced feed and water intakes.
- Increased defecation in the milking parlor.
- Increased incidences of mastitis.
- Elevated somatic cell counts (white blood cells in the milk).
- Increased still births.
- Calves born crippled.
- Calves born blind.
- Sickly newborn calves.
- Calves dying within several days of birth.
- Crippled cows.
- Joint problems.
- Behavioral changes.
- Anxiety.
- Nervousness.
- Fatigue.
- Depression.
- Poor hair coats.
- Poor reproductive performance.
- Increased aborted pregnancies.
- Reduction in milk output.
- Depressed immune systems.
- Increased death rates.

In the human, the effects appear to be very similar:

- Changed personality.

- Degrading mental health.

- Forgetfulness.

- Anger.

- Irritability.

- Anxiety.

- Fatigue.

- Eye problems.

- Nerve tingling.

- Itchy skin.

- Joint problems, especially the hips, knees and ankles.

- Arthritis symptoms.

- Aching bones.

- Sexual problems.

- Suicide.

- The problems may appear to be seasonal or related to the time of day.

- Cancer, Fibromyalgia, Multiple Scleroses and Chronic Fatigue Syndrome are suspected to be linked to it.

The emissions from AC electricity is added to by the extensive wireless communications in use in the city environment. You will see dense concentrations of wireless transmitters in the downtown areas. Further afield, you will see transmitters on government and commercial buildings. Cell phone towers litter the landscape every few miles. High powered weather and airport radar systems are present in every major city.

People commonly have many wireless devices in the form of cell phones, wireless networks, cordless phones, outdoor weather stations, radio controlled toys, and so on. Many people do not even realize that the utilities have installed wireless devices at their properties in the form of Smart/AMR/AMI utility meters. "Smart Meter Sickness" is now a medical diagnosis, although not formally recognized at the time of writing! Many homes today are the equivalent of antenna parks. Indeed, many electromagnetic radiation researchers call WiFi "the cell phone tower within your home". You can find higher radiation levels near these units than you can find near cell phone towers!

Male impotence is on the rise and so are the sales of impotence curing drugs. The impotence effect was noted to occur in RADAR workers during its development. Cell phones use RADAR frequencies, as does WiFi, and most domestic wireless products. It is likely that these wireless energies are contributing to the emasculation of the modern man.

Wireless radiation is readily absorbed by the human. The human is 70% to 90% water and the microwaves that are in the environment react with water. In the communications industry, this is called "Rain Fade". When it rains, the wireless radiation power levels reduce as the rain drops absorb the energy. The human body does the same thing!

When queried about how wireless radiation affects the human mind and body, the wireless radiation industry will commonly incorrectly state that the "skin effect" protects the human. The skin effect is an observation that high frequency currents will travel down the outside of a conductor and not the center of it. This effect was noticed during the development of high frequency electricity. Melanoma is linked to the high frequency skin effect.

The human body is not a conductor, but rather a semiconductor. Different electrical process are taking place and it is clear today that the human mind and body can be greatly affected by these high frequency man-made exposures. The human skin evolved in a natural

electromagnetic radiation environment and is now in a very unnatural man-made one that is making many people sick.

These harmful effects can be shown by growing plants in the electromagnetic fields. Dr. John Nash Ott extensively pioneered the field of electromagnetic radiation plant growth defects and his books on the subject are an interesting read. Like Dr. John Nash Ott, I have been able to deform plants with electromagnetic fields. This is what I have established:

- Found that Smart/AMR/AMI utility transmitting meters can have a toxic effect on the various biological systems that are near to them. The harmful biological effects can occur for at least 76 feet from some of the devices and can kill plants.

- Found that the radiation emissions from certain ionizing smoke detectors can retard cellular growth and may actually kill certain types of plants.

- Found that wireless radiation puts plants into a dormant state where they follow the changes in the seasons but do not actually grow or bear fruits. They become sterile and stunted. Removing the wireless radiation exposures resurrects them.

- Found that wireless radiation affects the growth and branching structure of some plants. Plants that grow tall may instead grow low to the ground.

- Some vines will not grow into areas of biologically unnatural radiation.

- Found that wireless radiation fields are patchy and unpredictable. Just moving a few inches can be the difference between a plant being healthy or it being stunted and deformed.

- Found that pulsed radiation from wireless weather station sensors and wireless utility meters can really retard and deform plants that are close to them. In some cases they will kill the plants.

- Discovered that certain electromagnetic exposures deform and retard plant growth and when removed, the plant drops all of the previous deformed leaf growth and starts growing normal growth from the tips of electromagnetic exposed part of the plant. The previously exposed part of the plant stays bald.

- Discovered that certain plants in unnatural radiation fields will only grow leaves on their branch tips at the edge of the plant. The interior of the branches of the plant stay bald. This growth pattern rectifies itself when the unnatural radiation field is removed.

- Found that the pomegranate tree will drop all of its leaf growth when the harmful wireless radiation field is removed and put up new growth from its base. The existing branches stay bald. The following year, it will put new leaf growth on both the old and new branches and bear fruit.

- Found that certain plants in biologically unnatural electromagnetic fields will turn their normally patterned leaves into dark green glossy leaves with no patterning.

It appears that when analyzing wireless radiation exposures you should think of them as you would think of a Tesla coil. The Tesla coil was where wireless radiation devices were developed from. A Tesla coil can emit biologically harmful visible sparks over long distances, often exceeding 100 feet. Some electrical, electronic, and wireless devices appear to emit similar biologically harmful "invisible sparks" a comparable distance. I call this:

"The Tesla Coil Model of Biologically Harmful Invisible Electromagnetic Radiation"

The human mind and body cannot sense these biologically harmful invisible sparks and it slowly gets sick from exposure to them. The longer you are exposed to it, the more toxic you become. The range of these toxic electromagnetic fields varies with each device and is very unpredictable.

The leaf defects that the Dieffenbachia (Dumb Cane) plant displays in unnatural electromagnetic fields are shown in the following picture.

Leaf Deformities

The fully grown leaf deformities are shown. As you can see, a wide range of different size leaves can be generated, depending on the field type and strength that the Dieffenbachia (Dumb Cane) plant is exposed to.

Regarding wireless transmitting devices, I have found after many plant growth experiments:

- Near exposures to transmitters are the most harmful. The most harmful transmitters that I have found are the lowest power ones that are sold to consumers as harmless wireless products! Devices that continually broadcast pulses of radiation every several seconds are the worst, such as wireless weather station sensors.

- Intermediate exposures are those from your neighbors wireless devices and those from Smart/AMR/AMI utility meters. These are the next worst exposures and you should be familiar with the wireless products that your neighbors have at their properties. You should consider installing electromagnetic shielding between the homes if they have harmful wireless products in use.

- Far exposures are those that are coming from high powered transmitters that are far away from your property. Examples of these are airport, port, and weather RADAR systems, TV and radio transmitters, government transmitters, cell phone towers, and so on. You should be aware of the locations of these to both your home and workplace. Only after working through the near and intermediate exposures should you start suspecting these as sources of your problems. Distance is your friend in the world of harmful electromagnetic radiation exposures!

My research is indicating that home wireless devices can produce a biologically toxic field close to them. The size of this harmful field varies from device to device. Some of the harmful fields from home devices can extend at least 76 feet and the field is very patchy. Some areas are really biologically toxic. Regarding the toxicity of wireless radiation exposures from common devices in the home, a clear classification is now emerging about the level of toxicity of these devices.

The most biologically harmful fields appear to be produced by pulsed radiation devices that broadcast regularly. Smart/AMR/AMI utility meters and wireless outdoor temperature sensors are good examples. "Smart" enabled devices that are designed to integrate into your utility "Smart" meter are likely to behave in a similar fashion. Some WiFi devices and smart phones also display this behavior and it may be related to the applications that they have installed on them. Automatic door opening RADAR sensors that are common in large stores may fall into this category. Security door and active animal tracking radio-frequency identification (RFID) tags are in this category.

After this, I have WiFi router exposure rated as the next most toxic device as it is broadcasting continuously in the home and workplace, make sure you do not sit near to them. You should use your computer on a wired network connection whenever possible and turn off the WiFi. Some cordless home phones may be in this category as they appear to behave like wireless networks. Wireless game controllers and radio controlled toys are in this category.

The cell phone is in the third class of toxic devices and I recommend people to avoid them. They communicate with the cell phone tower every ten minutes or so. Each time they do so, they will fill your home with wireless radiation. If you have multiple phones in the home, then your home will be filled with wireless radiation every few minutes. Some types of cordless home phones may fall into this category.

The fourth class of wireless device appears to be devices that only broadcast a short wireless pulse when they sense an event that triggers them. A garage door open or closed sensor would fall into this category. Most wireless security sensors and wireless door chimes behave in the same way. Some wireless utility meters also can exhibit this behavior.

This is the classification that appears to be emerging for home wireless devices from most toxic to least toxic:

1. **Devices that emit regular pulses of wireless radiation at short intervals of every 60 seconds or less.**

2. **Devices that constantly emit wireless radiation.**

3. **Devices that emit pulses of wireless radiation every several minutes.**

4. **Devices that emit pulses of wireless radiation infrequently.**

If you have several wireless devices close together, then you may have to reassess which category they fall into as it will increase the frequency of wireless pulses and wireless energy power being transmitted.

The frequency that a wireless device operates on may increase the toxicity of it. The most toxic device I identified at my home was a wireless outdoor temperature and humidity sensor. It operates for about a year on two AA 1.5 volt batteries. The frequency that it operated at was 433.92 megahertz and it appeared to be deforming a wide range of plants for at least a 45 feet radius from the device.

The gas company later installed an Itron 100G gas meter that surpassed the biological toxicity of that device to the human. Installed 76 feet away from my bedroom, that device induced classic Radio Wave Sickness into me! It is listed as operating at between 908 to 924 megahertz at up to half a watt of transmission power. Half a watt is high powered for a residential application that constantly transmits pulsed radiation every several seconds. It is unfortunate that the highest powered transmitting devices at your home may actually be the utility meters that you cannot switch off!

The Itron Centron, 40G and 100G utility meters become really biologically toxic when the utility meter reading car comes through the neighborhood. It has a high

powered transmitter on it that triggers all of the Itron utility meters in the area to transmit. This is by far the most biologically toxic human radio frequency exposure that I have come across in three years of radio frequency biological research. It is orders of magnitude more toxic than anything I have experienced during my research. You should avoid being outdoors in the sidewalk on the day that your transmitting utility meters are being read by the utility company meter reading car. It is actually preferable to go into the countryside on this day to avoid the spike in radiation levels. Many people will show adverse health conditions to this exposure that may last up to a week and the long term damage is currently unknown. The utilities willfully irradiating pregnant ladies, babies and developing children in their own residential sidewalks with known biologically toxic radiation probably will go down in history as one of their greatest crimes against humanity. I would recommend that you get familiar with the following: Smart Meter Opposition Groups in the United States of America http://www.takebackyourpower.net/directory/us/

To sum up, the biological toxicity of a transmitter to a human depends on the following:

- Transmission power.
- Transmitting frequency.
- Modulation of the signal.
- Intermittent, pulsed or continuous transmission.
- Reflections and interference of the transmission.
- Distance from the base station.
- Distance from you.
- Number and types of transmitters already installed into your area.
- The number, sizes and types of metals implanted into the human body.

- Your muscle mass.

- Your physical size.

- Your age.

- Your diet.

- Your past irradiation history.

- Metal jewelery.

- For the female: metal intrauterine devices (IUD) and metal bra under wires are likely to increase the risks.

Reasonable distances to stay away from transmitting devices to reduce the known health risks that they present are:

- **High powered RADAR: 20 miles.**

- **TV or radio transmitter: 5 miles.**

- **USA large city downtown area: 5 miles.**

- **Port, airport or military base: 5 miles.**

- **Cell phone tower: 1 mile.**

- **Police or hospital transmitters: 1 mile.**

- **Transmitting utility meters: Quarter of a mile.**

- **Active RFID devices: 100 feet.**

- **WiFi router: 50 feet.**

Cell phones become more hazardous the further away from the cell tower you are, as they have an automatic transmission power control feature on them to prolong battery life. When they are near to the cell tower they transmit at low power and when they are far away, they transmit at high power. If you only have one bar displaying in your phone signal strength meter, it is likely that your phone is transmitting at the highest power level and may actually be quite hazardous to you and the people around you!

Stadiums, cinema's and densely packed cubicle offices appear to be quite hazardous due to the high power levels that many cellphones create when transmitting. The largest stadiums in the USA can hold over 100,000 people and there may be a similar number of cellphones in there. That means that a packed stadium with 100,000 cellphones has the transmission power of approximately 200,000 watts of wireless energy!!! It has been noticed that American football players are developing strange brain cancers and it may be related to this effect. Unfortunately, I have not seen any studies of similar aged regular game spectators that carry cellphones and their brain cancer types and levels. It is prudent to avoid large groupings of people in a cell phone society. The medical profession will likely call this:

Dense Population Syndrome

You should be very wary of where you keep your cellphone and men should avoid keeping it near to their testicles and women should avoid keeping it near to the breasts. You should avoid putting a cellphone in your shirt pocket or bra as it will be irradiating your breasts, heart and lungs. You most certainly do not want to sleep with your cellphone under your pillow, but unfortunately, many children do this every night. It is preferable to carry a cellphone in a separate bag away from the body. It is important to note that many cellphone manufacturers now state in their phone manuals that it must be kept away from the body by approximately half an inch for safety. This is in contrast to most people that I observe holding the phone against their heads while talking, there is no space. When in the home, use it on speakerphone and keep it far away from the bedrooms.

It is interesting to note that astronomers have always thought that a mass human radiation extinction would come from a solar flare or a supernova. Pulsars may present the biggest naturally occurring risk to human extinction, as they

behave like pulsed wireless transmitters. As we know today, the pulsar radiation emission is far more harmful at much lower power levels than the continuous radiation emissions from the Sun or supernovas. This opens up the range of nearby astronomical objects that can threaten the Earth by orders of magnitude. As such, a human radiation extinction is far more likely to come from a pulsar than any other astronomical object!

When we talk about extinction, we must remember that this will also affect everything on the Earth. Human survival is completely dependent on plants. Plants are affected by many forms of radiation and I have performed numerous tests that show the biologically harmful effects from man-made radiation exposures, as has Dr. John Nash Ott.

Regarding the toxicity of wireless radiation exposures, this is the official stance currently:

Lyon, France, May 31, 2011: The WHO/International Agency for Research on Cancer (IARC) has classified radio frequency electromagnetic fields as possibly carcinogenic to humans (Group 2B), based on an increased risk for glioma, a malignant type of brain cancer, associated with wireless phone use.

I have found climbing vines will not grow into areas of harmful wireless radiation and that the Golden Pothos will lose the patterning on its leaves in these fields. This is shown in the following pictures.

Golden Pothos

The Golden Pothos will lose the patterning in its leaves when in harmful wireless radiation fields. They grow dark green.

Climbing Vines

Some climbing vines will not grow into harmful wireless radiation areas. They provide an excellent indicator of the invisible patches of harmful wireless radiation that now exist.

Electrical energy interacts with the natural fields of the Earth. The human is genetically adapted to interact with natural, weak magnetic and electromagnetic fields. The cities represent the opposite of what nature created and today are an alien environment for the modern human. As such, it is reasonable to say that the modern human is an alien having developed in such an alien environment.

The alien human is revealing itself in many ways. We can see it in the dramatic rise in childhood development problems. Autism, attention deficit disorder, hyperactivity, insomnia, depression, fatigue, aggression and accelerated puberty are all problems that are prevalent in modern children. Autism is the most striking and has accelerated from being a rare problem in the 1970's where only 1 in 10,000 children were diagnosed with the condition to a common development issue where 1 in 40 boys have it today!

Autism has been following the rise in wireless communications for the last decade and this is shown in the next graph. The graph was complied from data presented by CTIA-The Wireless Association and Talk About Curing Autism (TACA). It is clearly an electromagnetic radiation disease. The longer the damaging effects of man-made electromagnetic radiation are denied, the more this graph will continue to increase. Unfortunately, the wireless radiation era is not a good time to be born into.

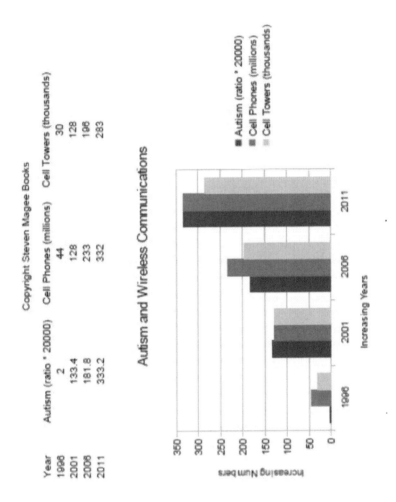

Copyright Steven Magee Books

Year	Autism (ratio * 20000)	Cell Phones (millions)	Cell Towers (thousands)
1998	2	44	30
2001	133.4	128	128
2006	181.8	233	196
2011	333.2	332	283

Autism and Wireless Communications

The BioInititaive 2012 report states:

The premise of this review is that although scant attention has been paid to possible links between electromagnetic fields and radiofrequency exposures (EMF/RFR) and Autism Spectrum Disorders (ASDs), such links probably exist. The rationale for this premise is that the physiological impacts of EMF/RFR and a host of increasingly well-documented pathophysiological phenomena in ASDs have remarkable similarities.

Loops are present throughout the human body and some are obvious and others are more discrete. Some of the places that you will find loops in the human body are:

- Inner Ear.
- Eye pupil.
- Eye orbit.
- Nostril.
- Spinal column.
- Collar bone.
- Circular bone surrounding marrow.
- Heart.
- Rib cage.
- Intestines.
- Kidneys.
- Ovaries and fallopian tubes.
- Hips.
- Blood cells.
- Arteries, veins, and capillaries.

Why are loops a concern? Because they may couple into the electrical fields by a process called "induction". Induction may cause electrical currents to flow within the loops when in the presence of frequency fields. Flowing currents through these loops may cause illness and disease to occur. The currents may cause localized heating, electric and magnetic fields.

Regarding the blood, the cells are known to stick together in long chains when in unnatural electromagnetic fields. The effect is known as a "rouleaux formation" and it can be undone by exposing the blood to natural sunlight.

Man-made loops may be present on the human body and we see these in various locations:

- Eye wear.
- Earrings.
- Necklace.
- Rings.
- Bangles.
- Bracelets.
- Watches.

You should also be wary of any kind of metal on the human body. In particular, the curved metal wire in under-wired bra's has already been identified to be acting as a reflector for focusing radio and microwaves into the breast tissue. Breast cancer is on the rise in young ladies who carry cellphones in their bras and the risk is increased if they have a history of chest X-rays as a teenager. Metal zippers can have similar focusing effects. The next diagram shows this effect.

A similar effect to the under-wired bra may occur in the astronomical field, but on a much larger scale. Metal observatory domes may act as reflectors that focus radio and microwaves. Any curved metal structure may exhibit this focusing effect. You should not use transmitting devices in such environments. This is shown in the following diagram.

Any metal structure may be able to cause radio and microwave reflections to occur and you should be wary of using products that create electromagnetic waves in locations such as these.

Focusing Radiation with an Under Wired Bra

Electromagnetic interference, radio and microwaves

High radiation zone

High radiation zone

Metal Dome Radiation Reflections

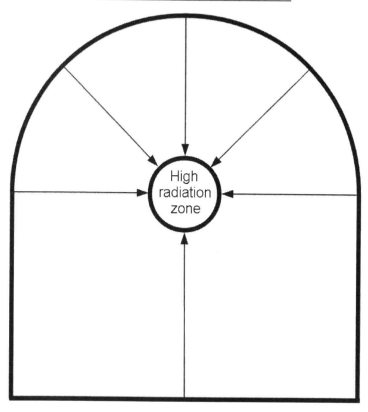

Any transmitting device in the center of the dome will create a high radiation area from the reflected waves

The human nervous system never connects in a loop and this is probably to prevent electrical induction effects from occurring in it. Instead the nerves are balanced between the left and right side of the human body, feeding out radially from the spinal cord to the various bodily systems that they connect to.

High powered alternating current electricity does not occur in nature and it is wise to exercise caution around it. There must be a reason why nature does not use it and it would be foolish to ignore this. All high powered electricity in nature is direct current (DC). The electric eel is a good example of this and it can generate a voltage of approximately 500 volts to stun its prey. Thunderstorms also produce large DC voltages of millions of volts and we see this as lightning. It appears that Edison was right to promote the use of DC electricity in the famous "War of the Currents" that he had with Tesla's AC system.

Radio waves do occur in nature and these generally are seasonal with the arrival of lighting storms. It appears that the radio waves that nature produces are a stimulant to the human mind and body for fertility and also sexual desire. Given that humans have now filled their environments with radio waves all year round, it should come as no surprise that we have seen unprecedented growth in human population over the last century. The human body may now be extremely fertile all year, as opposed to the fertility and mating cycles following the seasons in the past.

Fortunately, the human mind and body does appear to have an electrical noise reduction system built into its nervous system. The nervous system is widely acknowledged to be driven by electrical impulses, so this is not a surprise. The left part of the brain controls the right side of the body and the right part of the brain controls the left side of the body. This twist that occurs appears to be an electrical noise reduction technique that enables the body to function in high EMI environments. This is shown in the next diagram.

Human Body Electromagnetic Field Cancellation

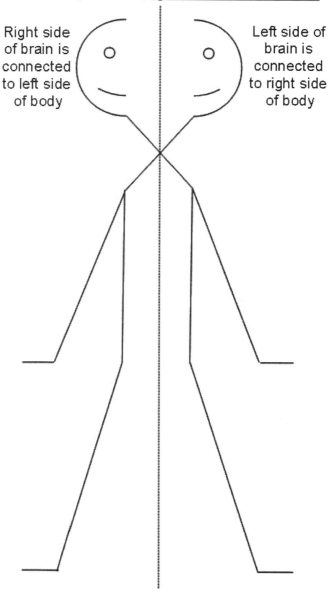

Right side of brain is connected to left side of body

Left side of brain is connected to right side of body

The nervous system uses electrical noise reduction techniques

The back and forth structures of the brain and intestines may also be an electrical noise canceling technique. The arteries and veins generally run next to each other and this is another electrical noise reduction effect. The double helix spiral in DNA creates electromagnetic shielding and nullification effects. Electrical noise reduction techniques are present throughout the body.

There are certain parts of the body that may act like antennas and these may be:

- Brain.
- Body.
- Spinal cord.
- Intestines.
- Arms.
- Legs.
- Digits.
- Hair.

It is well known that when the human is placed into an unnatural electromagnetic environment that this affects the intestinal flora. The intestines are filled with digestive microbes and the growth of these can either be retarded or accelerated by the electromagnetic fields that they are in. Retardation will bring about poor digestion and acceleration will bring on excessive gas due to overgrowth inside the intestines. I experienced the gassy overgrowth effect in one of my jobs when I was sitting next to an electrical room daily.

Fertility appears to improve away from wireless technologies. Before trying to get pregnant, I recommend that people clean up their electromagnetic environments to give their children the best chance of going to the full term of 9 months and being born into an environment that is conducive to their healthy development.

Royal Raymond Rife (May 16, 1888 – August 5, 1971) was developing frequencies of energy for medical treatments. He found that certain frequencies would alleviate certain conditions. His work appeared to evolve into what we now know today as transcutaneous electrical nerve stimulation (TENS) devices that are used to heal and radio frequency therapy that produces deep heating in the body tissues and stimulates collagen tightening, repair and regeneration.

If we take a look at the history of EMI we can see that there are definite steps in the progression of it throughout society:

- 1800's-1860's: Telegraph development. Joseph Henry invents the electric doorbell.

- 1870's: Thomas Edison develops the phonograph and starts manufacturing light bulbs. Alexander Graham Bell patents the telephone. Henry dies, aged 80.

- 1880's: Edison and Nikola Tesla are developing their electrical distribution systems. Edison sets up the first electrical utility using a 110 volt direct current (DC) system in New York City. More than 150,000 USA people are using telephones.

- 1890's: Oil and gas were starting to replace coal and wood. X-rays discovered. Tesla sets up the first alternating current (AC) utility in Niagara Falls.

- 1900's: Cars and airplanes were developing with electrical ignition systems. Most homes have electric doorbells.

- 1910's: Radio is being developed. First World War. Tesla's mental health is degrading and he is having financial problems.

- 1920's: Widespread adoption of Tesla's alternating current electrical system in cities. Leukemia is appearing in the population. The mass population is being exposed to electric lights and cinema. Bell dies, aged 75.

- 1930's: Widespread adoption of radio. RADAR and jet engine is in development. Edison dies, aged 84.

- 1940's: Widespread adoption of the alternating current (AC) electrical system in farming communities. Second World War. Development of nuclear bombs and worldwide dispersal of man-made fall-out radiation. Tesla dies, aged 86.

- 1950's: Development of the transistor and nuclear power. Extensive air testing of nuclear bombs and worldwide radiation fallout. Dr. John Nash Ott is discovering many detrimental health effects of electromagnetic radiation.

- 1960's: Widespread adoption of televisions and cars. The modern computer is being developed. The Space industry is being developed. The medical profession is trying to understand organ failure. Nuclear bomb testing moved underground to prevent worldwide radiation dispersal. Dr. John Nash Ott is discovering X-ray emissions from florescent lights and televisions.

- 1970's: Widespread use of digital watches and calculators. Adoption of international jet travel. Many communications satellites are now in orbit. Smooth float glass is becoming common in buildings. Color television became popular. Dr. John Nash Ott is discovering that electrical lighting products are changing the gender of animals and plants.

- 1980's: Widespread adoption of home and business computers, video games, video recorders and portable cassette players. Typical microprocessor speed of 1Mhz. Satellite television is in homes, as are radioactive ionizing smoke detectors. Diabetes is widespread. Cell phone towers are being constructed. Dr. John Nash Ott is discovering that the new electronic products are causing health problems in humans. Florescent lighting products are inducing cancer into his laboratory rats.

- 1990's: Widespread adoption of digital electronics into the home and workplace. Typical processor speed of 10Mhz. Cordless home and business phones that use radio frequencies are becoming popular. Coated double glazed glass is becoming commonplace in homes and businesses. RADAR systems are in use in commercial applications and weather forecasting. Autism is starting to become prevalent. Construction of International Space Station (ISS) is started. Rapid construction of cell phone towers is significantly raising the radiation levels. Dr. John Nash Ott is failing in his efforts to get his findings out to the mainstream population, media organizations will not report it.

- 2000's: Internet was widely adopted and much of commerce became conducted using it. Laptop computers and cellphones became popular. Typical processor speed of 100Mhz. Ionizing smoke detectors are installed in every bedroom. Electrical outlets are now installed every ten feet in homes. Obesity epidemic underway. Bee colonies are collapsing around the world. Fraudulent invasions of countries. Dr. John Nash Ott dies after much of his work is willfully ignored by the government, corporations, media, and research institutions.

- 2010's: GPS systems, tablet computers and smart phones became popular. Almost all young children now have cellphones, computers, and electrical and electronic toys. Children's game consoles now have wireless radiation controllers. Typical processor speed of 1 Ghz. Breast cancer is affecting 1 in 8 women. Almost all types of cancer are increasing. Autism and Attention Deficit Disorder (ADD) are widespread. Atmospheric carbon dioxide is double the historical records. Construction of the International Space Station is completed and it is the largest man-made object in orbit. The Earth is ringed in thousands of man-made satellites that are regularly eclipsing the Sun. The sky is filled with chemical trails from jet aircraft that linger for hours. Cirrus clouds have become prevalent. Cell phone coverage of 99% of the USA population is achieved with many people in multiple cell phone system transmission areas. Homes and workplaces have been turned into high powered antenna parks with the installation of radiation transmitting Smart/AMR/AMI utility meters and people are getting sick from them. The next generation of weather RADAR systems are installed into USA cities. The human electromagnetic radiation environment has never existed in the history of the world. The USA is calling itself "The Greatest Nation on Earth".

So as we can see, electromagnetic interference has been constantly changing over the last two centuries to the point where we are immersed in electromagnetic interference fields that are a soup of various forms of radiation. The biggest man-made experiment on the Earth is in full swing and you are a part of it!

So how do you prevent electromagnetic interference? The main thing that you can do is reduce your exposure by switching off as much of your electrical, electronic and wireless products as possible. You should also identify how much electromagnetic interference each of your products emits. A simple AM radio tuned to static (no radio station) can detect most electromagnetic interference fields and they are strongest at the equipment and fade with distance. De-clutter your home from these products and just have the products that you really need. Naturally, your bedrooms should be free of any electromagnetic interference producing equipment. If you are going to use electromagnetic interference producing equipment, then you should be using low electromagnetic interference versions of it wherever possible. You should consider switching off the electrical circuit breakers for rooms that you do not use and also the bedrooms. It is a good idea not to be exposed to AC electrical fields while you are sleeping. Some people actually turn off their electrical fuse board when they go to bed to effect this.

Have an electrician check your electrical ground, plumbing ground, conductive flooring, water systems, drains, and garden for stray voltage and dirty electricity effects.

If you are serious about eliminating the sources of electromagnetic interference then you may want to obtain the following items of test equipment to aid with diagnosing problems (My test equipment is in brackets):

- A portable, battery powered analogue AM radio (Sharper Image Model GFSI-0100).

- A digital multimeter with a minimum and maximum feature (Amprobe 5XP-A).

- A magnetic field, electric field, and microwave field meter (TriField Model 100XE).

- A low frequency magnetic field detector (Telephone voice pickup coil connected to a battery powered amplified speaker.)

- A battery powered oscilloscope with a Fast Fourier Transform function (FFT) (Owon PDS 5022S).

- A three axis RF meter (Tenmars TM-196).

- A battery powered LASER and RADAR detector (Whistler XTR 445).

You should make yourself aware of the peak load times of the electrical systems in your area and see if they coincide with health problems occurring:

- Air conditioning loads of summertime.

- Heating loads of wintertime.

- Industrial area load peaks are 08:00 to 17:00.

- Residential area load peaks are 16:00 to 20:00.

- Solar power systems turn on shortly after sunrise and turn off shortly before sunset with peak power being midday. On a day with broken clouds, they will produce rapid energy swings on the electricity system that will modulate the current flow in the area which may produce frequency emissions on associated electrical equipment. This effect is known to make some solar photovoltaic workers mentally and physically sick and is likely to become known as "Solar Photovoltaic Syndrome".

- Wind power peaks will coincide with the rising wind speed in the area. Wind power systems typically turn on at approximately 12 miles per hour (MPH) and generally don't make much power below 20 MPH wind speeds. They should generate significant electrical power above 30 MPH. Wind Turbine Syndrome is now a documented health condition that may occur in areas that have wind turbines installed. Denmark is considered to be the home of the wind turbine and it has seen a recent spike in its breast cancer and melanoma rates that may be related to the large number of wind turbines in that country.

You should also pay attention to where you spend time and how you feel in those environments. A long drive may bring on symptoms from exposure to car electromagnetic interference and pollution. Time spent at your job may bring on symptoms from either Sick Building Syndrome or pollution that your job exposes you to. Your employer may be avoiding informing you of known hazards of your job, as they may have seen the same thing with previous employees and know that the job is hazardous to human health. You may be the latest employee getting sick out of the many people who came before you!

It is an unfortunate state of affairs that we find ourselves having to do the governments job of protecting ourselves from known harm. Electrical, electronic and wireless equipment should never have been allowed into the home or workplace that may cause harm to human health. It is a sign that self regulation by industries does not work and that profits have been put before human health. With the recent environmental disasters of Hurricane Katrina in 2005, the BP Deepwater Horizon gulf oil spill in 2010 and the Fukushima nuclear disaster in 2011, we can see that the modern government systems of public protection are failing.

In this "modern" society, it is clear that you are responsible for your own health. Ultimately, if you have EHS, you may have to move to the countryside to a known low electromagnetic interference area if you are unable to clean up your environment sufficiently. Trees are excellent at suppressing electromagnetic interference due to their effective grounding. They essentially are nature's version of the Faraday Cage that is used to suppress electromagnetic interference in the engineering field.

An interesting fact that bears some thought are the differences that were observed in Edison and Tesla. Edison was developing a direct current (DC) electrical system and Tesla was developing an alternating current (AC) system. Edison was regarded as a respected businessman, while Tesla was regarded as a mad scientist. It is quite possible that the mental issues that Tesla displayed had come from exposure to his work with alternating current. Direct current that Edison was working with does not transmit through the air as well. Both men lived into their 80's and Edison was experimenting with dietary intake towards the end of his life, presumably to cure his ailments. Perhaps Edison had become a victim of exposure to Tesla's alternating current system, the very system that he had lobbied against as being a danger to human health!

It is unfortunate that these electromagnetic interference effects have occurred and we may now have widespread electrical poisoning in the modern world. An electrically poisoned human is not going to think normally nor function normally. When you observe the modern population you can see that there are many different personalities around, many of which do not appear to be normal and it is probably a sign of poisoning.

Humans are displaying an addiction to electrical energy that appears to be like drug addiction. It rules their lives. Humans should be weaned off electrical energy consumption in order to reduce this unnatural dependance that has been formed. Homes should have trees placed around them to help keep them cool and reduce the air conditioning loads on the electrical grid. Ideally, homes should be located under the tree canopy.

The human mind and body cannot sense most forms of radiation. It slowly gets sick from exposure to biologically harmful forms of it. Harmful radiation comes in many forms in society:

Radio frequencies have become a plague in modern society. Many conditions are linked to it including Autism and Attention Deficit Disorder. Are you being affected? Radio Wave Sickness is well categorized today and the top reported Radio Wave Sickness symptoms in order of frequency are: Fatigue, sleep disturbance, headaches, feeling of discomfort, difficulty in concentrating, depression, memory loss, visual disruptions, irritability, hearing disruptions, skin problems, cardiovascular, dizziness, loss of appetite, movement difficulties and nausea. (Source: Symptoms experienced by people in the vicinity of a cellular phone base station, Santini 2001, La Presse Medical.) Radio Wave Sickness is commonly referred to today as Electromagnetic Hypersensitivity and how high is too high for wireless radiation exposures? People with Electromagnetic Hypersensitivity commonly report the following: 6 to 3 V/m: Too high for ambient levels. 1 to 0.3 V/m: Too high for many people. 0.1 to 0.05 V/m: Many people have symptoms. 0.02 to 0.01 V/m: Most people with EHS are okay. (Source: EMFields Acousticom 2). The Tenmars TM-196 RF meter manual states *"We recommend a maximum level of 0.614 V/m for prolonged exposure"*. It is normal to find yourself sitting and walking around in fields of wireless radiation of approximately 1 V/m in the USA. Antenna systems are commonly unseen inside buildings and various products that professional testing can reveal their presence. Invisible transmitters are called "Stealth" systems in the industry.

RADAR is found in security sensors, traffic control systems and automatic doors on many shops. It can travel for quite some distance from the RADAR device. RADAR exposure is linked to cataracts, impotence and Radio Wave Sickness.

LASER is commonly found in speed control devices. The LASER beam can travel for long distances and may be pointing at your home or workplace. LASER exposure is known to affect the eyes.

Electric fields are found anywhere there are energized electrical cables. All cables emit them. The size of the electrical field can vary with the dirty electricity on the electrical system. You may get fatigued from electrical field exposure.

Magnetic fields are created by current flow through electrical cables and they are known for their ability to affect the human mind. Strange psychological issues may show up. You will find these in your home, your workplace, your car, public transportation systems and near to power lines. Ground loops are a common problem and if you have one in your home, it may be comparable to living under a power line.

Electrostatic fields are found near to power lines. This is the field that will make the hair on your body react and stand up. It is generated by high rates of change of voltage. People who live in homes that have this field in them may slowly get sick.

Ionizing radiation sources are found in smoke detectors, X-Ray machines and some industrial meters. They are to be avoided. Ionizing radiation is regarded as the most biologically harmful form of radiation and comes from nuclear reactors.

Stray voltage/current/frequencies comes from electrical grounding systems and is known for its ability to significantly affect human health. In the home it is typically seen to electrify conductive tile and concrete flooring, metal cases of appliances, drains and the water systems of the home. Just 0.5 volt of AC electricity is known for its harmful effects on biological systems. The latest research is indicating that biological issues are being seen at just 0.01 volt of AC stray voltage exposure.

Ultraviolet (UV) and Infrared (IR) exposures come in two forms and these are increased or decreased exposures. Increased exposures occur on the outside of reflective buildings and from some types of electrical lighting products. Decreased exposure comes from filtered light through windows and also from electrical lighting products. Correct selection of electrical lighting products and window types is important in preventing Sick Building Syndrome from occurring. Dr. John Nash Ott reported cells would rupture when exposed to too much UV. This famous quote summarizes his findings: "Mal-illumination is to light as malnutrition is to food."

Electromagnetic Interference (EMI) comprises of all of the above exposures. EMI is known for its harmful health effects and is poorly regulated in the USA. There are many biologically toxic products on sale that may make you sick with long term exposure to them. EMI is so good at making people sick that the modern military weaponized it decades ago and calls them "Electromagnetic Weapons" or "Silent Weapons".

One of the beneficial effects of electromagnetic radiation are the naturally occurring Schumann Resonances. People report the use of electromagnetic waves as being beneficial to health and these devices are commonly called "Schumann Resonators" that put out the natural Schumann Resonance of 7.83 Hz. I have not met anyone yet who has successfully applied Schumann Resonances to alleviate their health conditions. I investigated the application of Schumann Resonances to the human through to the eighth harmonic and did not reach any definite conclusions. However, I have grown plants inside of a Faraday cage with a radiation source and they showed beneficial growth patterns when compared to Faraday cage plants without the radiation source. This is in line with the belief that the International Space Station has a Schumann Resonator installed in it to keep the astronauts healthy.

I applied the Schumann Resonances to the human mind by using standard electrical headphones connected to an MP3 player. The soundtrack that I developed is available commercially and is called "7.83Hz Schumann Resonance to the Eighth Harmonic". It contains harmonics of the original fundamental frequency through to the eighth. Tracks with harmonics 1, 2 or 3 may not be audible, but do produce the electromagnetic wave from the coils inside the headphones.

You need to be careful with electrical headphones, as you are applying an electromagnetic wave to the human brain. You should avoid using electrical headphones and use either speakers or air tube headsets to listen to your music. Regarding speakers, make sure that you are sitting several feet away from them due to the magnetic and electromagnetic fields that come out of them.

When applying the Schumann Resonances through electrical headphones I did notice that my sleep patterns changed and I was waking up before sunrise for a few days. I also saw some strange nerve twitching in my shoulder and headaches that cleared up after several days of continued application of the soundtrack. There appeared to be no lasting effects after I stopped applying them after one month of daily application of the resonances for two hours a day. I stopped as I was not seeing any improvement in my energy levels.

To sum up this chapter, here are the suspected health hazards of electromagnetic interference:

- Direct contact with electricity system live conductors can cause electric shock, electrical burns, and possibly death.

- Corroded utility neutrals may shock and cause electrocution.

- A surge in stray voltage may cause human electrocution in swimming pools and wet areas.

- Long term exposure to stray voltage may cause human health to degrade.

- Long term exposure to electric fields may cause human health to degrade.

- Long term exposure to magnetic fields above 2 mill-gauss may cause human health to degrade.

- Long term exposure to radio or microwave fields may cause human health to degrade.

- Long term exposure to an ion field imbalance may cause human health to degrade.

- Long term exposure to power lines may cause human health to degrade.

- Long term exposure to electricity that contains harmonics and various frequencies (Dirty electricity) may cause human health to degrade.

- Nighttime exposure may be a higher risk, due to radio waves transmitting better during this time.

- Reduction or loss of atmospheric DC voltage may cause human health to degrade.

More details on this subject can be found in the following books:

The book "Toxic Electricity" presents an analysis of the toxicity of electricity, electronics and wireless radiation.

The health effects of the AC electricity system can be found in "Dirty Electricity: Electrification and the Diseases of Civilization." by Dr. Samuel Milham MD MPH. He notes that Leukemia is almost unknown in Africa where there is minimal electrification and the disease appears to be following the progress of electrification. It was unknown by the world medical profession until the 1920's when electricity started to become commonplace.

The Earth's ground is now very different and more on this subject can be found in the book "Earthing: The Most Important Health Discovery Ever?" by Clinton Ober, Stephen T. Sinatra MD, and Martin Zucker. You need to be very careful about connecting into the ground in developed environments that have electricity, as they may have energized the ground around the electrical systems. If the ground has been energized by AC electricity, then you may get very sick by being in contact with it. Earthing the human body to the electrical system and/or electrified earth and/or cables that have radio frequencies on them may be a risky activity for long term human health.

The book "Electrocution of America: Is Your Utility Out to Kill You?" by Russ Allen documents the detrimental health effects of stray voltage/current/frequencies in the ground.

Documentation regarding the rise of electromagnetic interference pollution can be found in the following books:

- "Cross Currents: The Perils of Electropollution" by Dr. Robert O. Becker.

- "Electromagnetic Fields: A Consumer's Guide to the Issue and How to Protect Ourselves" by B. Blake Levitt.

- "The Invisible Disease: The Dangers of Environmental Illnesses Caused by Electromagnetic Fields and Chemical Emissions" by Gunni Nordstrom.

- "The Force: Living Safely in a World of Electromagnetic Pollution." by Lyn McClean.

- "Silent Fields" and "Dirty Electricity and Electromagnetic Radiation" by Donna Fisher.

Biological defects associated with electromagnetic interference (EMI) can be found in "Light, Radiation, and You." by Dr. John N. Ott.

Human health issues in the electronics industry is well documented in "Challenging the Chip: Labor Rights and Environmental Justice in the Global Electronics Industry." by

Ted Smith, David A. Sonnenfeld, David Naguib Pellow, and Jim Hightower.

I can recommend the free BioInitiative 2012 report for further reading on the subject of wireless radiation:

http://www.bioinitiative.org/

Books that document the known biologically harmful effects of wireless radiation are:

- "Disconnect" by Devra Davis.
- "Public Health SOS: The Shadow Side of the Wireless Revolution" by Magda Havas and Camilla Rees.
- "Cellular Telephone Russian Roulette" by Robert Kane.

Dr. Magda Havas has an excellent electromagnetic website at: www.magdahavas.com

A nice list of research papers about "Dirty Electricity" and the effects on human health can be found at: http://www.stetzerelectric.com/researchPaper/list

Stray voltage reducing products are available and a popular product is the "Ronk Blocker" from Ronk Electrical Industries.

For detecting dirty electricity, Stetzer Electric have developed the "STETZERiZER Meter".

"All the things that human beings suffer from are how their environment treats them, and how the elements of their planet affects their mind and body - like radiation, cancer, and all."

Ornette Coleman

Metals

We cannot live without metals in our food and water. Metals provide the human mind and body the ability to generate DC voltage. Without the DC voltage we would eventually get sick. Metals have a wide range of functions in the biological system of the human and we are only at the start of understanding these processes. Mined and purified metals are the opposite and present a hazard to the human.

The use of metals is a very unnatural activity of the human. Metals are found dispersed in nature. They are generally mined from underground and many processes are used to extract them from the rock that they are part of. Once concentrated into pure metal, their interaction with the natural environment is greatly changed.

Wherever you find pure metals, you will also find very strange magnetic and electromagnetic fields. This is an issue as the human has not evolved in these strange fields. With the advent of electricity, electronics and wireless communications, there are now very strange electromagnetic radiation induced energies flowing in all metals. As such prolonged contact with metals is likely to be toxic to humans.

You should avoid metals in your home and workplace and instead be using wooden furniture where possible. Metal chairs are a bad idea and you should be sitting on wooden chairs. Metal coil mattresses are another item that you should be avoiding. Instead, you should be sleeping on mattresses made out of natural foam materials.

Metal jewelery should be avoided in a wireless radiation society. The worst form of jewelery is anything that is formed into a loop, as it will exhibit the electromagnetic induction effect that should enhance the energy being produced. Examples of these are rings, watches, necklaces, bangles, hoop earrings, and so on. Metal under wired bras and metal interuterine devices (IUD) should be avoided also.

Metal implants of any kind are a bad idea. Metal fillings, bridges, crowns, and implants should be avoided. If you have an accident and they fuse your bones together with metal, you should have the metal removed after you have healed. Hip implants are generally the largest piece of metal that you see in the human. People who have metal implants should be familiar with the symptoms of Electromagnetic Hypersensitivity and should keep their environment free of electromagnetic interference producing products.

Metal hip implants are already getting caught up in class action lawsuits for various reasons. It is only a matter of time before metal implant patients realize that they have an antenna system installed into them that also acts like an electrode of a battery. Metals installed into the body are likely to interfere with the natural DC voltage processes of the body and set up internal battery discharge currents.

"I have every expectation that we will see the following become a recognized human disease in the future: Metal Sickness"

Steven Magee

Altitude

I have a lot of experience with altitude. I spent three years working at approximately 7,775 feet followed by five years at 13,796 feet and three more years at 6,875 feet. Altitude sickness is very real and the effects that it can have on people are diverse. Feeling faint is a common symptom and I have seen people actually faint at altitude.

When I worked in La Palma in the Canary Islands at 7,775 feet, the observatory was significantly above the tree line. The tree line is located at a very definite altitude. Above it, the vegetation significantly changes to low bushy growth of only a couple of feet tall. The trees at the tree line tend to be disfigured and showing stress. This indicates that the biological environment has changed and is biologically harmful to trees. It is likely a solar radiation effect.

The Hawaii observatory was significantly higher at 13,796 feet. It was a barren place with almost no visible life where the observatory was located. Just lots of rocks and cinder! It was far above the tree line. Our blood oxygen levels would be running at 80% of normal up there.

The Arizona observatory at 6,875 feet was below the tree line. However, it appeared to be high enough to cause growth defects in the trees. I remember the trees up there being twisted and disfigured. You could definitely feel the altitude sickness even at this lower elevation.

Altitude sickness is known to occur in most people above 4,900 feet. Aircraft commonly pressurize their cabins to the air pressure found at 6,900 feet to try and prevent these symptoms from occurring. However, some people still report altitude sickness symptoms at this pressure. They are probably the ones that you see holding the sick bags! Nausea is a feature of altitude sickness.

There are very definite symptoms that are associated with the different levels of altitude and Wikipedia states:

- *High altitude 1,500 to 3,500 metres (4,900 to 11,500 ft) - The onset of physiological effects of diminished inspiratory oxygen pressure (PiO2) includes decreased exercise performance and increased ventilation (lower arterial PCO2). Minor impairment exists in arterial oxygen transport (arterial oxygen saturation (SaO2) at least 90%), but arterial PO2 is significantly diminished. Because of the large number of people who ascend rapidly to altitudes between 2,400 and 4,000 m, high-altitude illness is common in this range.*

- *Very high altitude 3,500 to 5,500 metres (11,500 to 18,000 ft) - Maximum SaO2 falls below 90% as the arterial PO2 falls below 60mmHg. Extreme hypoxemia may occur during exercise, during sleep, and in the presence of high altitude pulmonary edema or other acute lung conditions. Severe altitude illness occurs most commonly in this range.*

- *Extreme altitude above 5,500 metres (18,000 ft) - Marked hypoxemia, hypocapnia, and alkalosis are characteristic of extreme altitudes. Progressive deterioration of physiologic function eventually outstrips acclimatization. As a result, no permanent human habitation occurs above 6,000m. A period of acclimatization is necessary when ascending to extreme altitude; abrupt ascent without supplemental oxygen for other than brief exposures invites severe altitude sickness.*

The Hawaii observatory was so high that we used to stop and acclimatize at 9,200 feet, before heading to the peak.

I was lucky enough to have two positions in Hawaii. The first position had me commuting from sea level to 13,796 feet on a daily basis. I would feel lethargic, have a headache, and show stomach problems during the day. In the evening, I just wanted to lay down and recover. I changed my position to the night shift and found that it was much more agreeable to human health. Indeed, it was one of my motivations to move onto the night shift. On nights I would stay on the mountain at 9,200 feet for five nights and commute up to 13,796 feet to work.

One of the things that I do remember that was distinct about working nights at 13,796 feet were the hallucinations. I saw some strange things on top of that mountain! I knew I was hallucinating and it was manageable feature of my job. I found it absolutely fascinating to see the tricks that the human mind could play on me. It was not often that I would have hallucinations, but it generally would occur on my first night on the mountain where my environmental conditions had been greatly changed. Many people report feeling a "presence" when at high altitudes and I frequently experienced this sensation.

Common to all three observatories where I worked was that the long term staff appeared to get leg problems. Some of them would have very strange walks. Indeed, it was like being in the Monty Python's sketch of "The Ministry of Silly Walks"! It was as if their joints had gone stiff. They also did not appear to be very healthy. I suspect that it was caused by daily high altitude commuting and the strange environmental conditions that they were working in. This appears to be called "Delayed Radiation Myelopathy" and is well documented in the medical field of nuclear medicine.

I did see two of the long term full time mountain employees die of disease. These disease conditions that they had were preceded by many years of poor health and both had the strange walks that I was observing. I imagine that high altitude commuting increases the risks of illness, disease and premature death.

This leads me into the purpose of this chapter and that is as you increase in altitude, your environmental conditions significantly change. The higher you go, the greater the change is. There are a wide variety of changes that occur and we will look into these.

Temperature is the most obvious change. The higher you go, the cooler it gets. In Hawaii, you could be sunbathing in shorts on the beach in the morning and by the afternoon you would be in your winter clothes making snowmen on top of the mountain! The temperature change between sea level and 13,796 feet can be extreme.

Less noticeable is the change in solar radiation levels. The sunlight is stronger and has frequencies of radiation in it that you will never find at sea level. As such, the solar radiation conditions are unnatural to the human. We see the effects of this at the tree line in the stressed trees. The ultraviolet levels increase by approximately 10% to 12% with every increase of 3,281 feet in altitude.

If you were to take a Geiger counter to altitude, you would notice that there are far more counts per minute (CPM) on it. This is because the closer you get to Space, the higher the radioactivity from Space becomes! The difference between being below 4,900 feet and above 4,900 feet is significant. Cosmic radiation exposures approximately double with every four thousand feet increase in altitude. This is most certainly an issue for frequent air travelers. At 35 degrees north latitude we find the radiation levels at altitude are:

- **0 Feet = 0.04 micro Sieverts per hour.**
- **10,000 Feet = 0.19 micro Sieverts per hour.**
- **20,000 Feet = 0.99 micro Sieverts per hour.**
- **30,000 Feet = 3.25 micro Sieverts per hour.**
- **40,000 Feet = 6.68 micro Sieverts per hour.**

Nighttime radiation levels are different also. Less atmospheric filtering is taking place and the radiation levels from Space are much higher. You actually see less stars up there, due to the eyes being starved of oxygen. They lose some of their nighttime sensitivity.

Radiation from artificial satellites is greatly increased due to the thinner atmosphere absorbing less artificial radiation. You will be exposed to much higher radio frequencies from the global positioning system (GPS), communication satellites and RADAR mapping satellites. LASER mapping satellites will expose you to higher levels of their radiation. I was a little surprised to find that my cell phone would work at 13,796 feet and it indicates that ground based transmitters are extensively radiating out to Space.

The electrical conductivity of the air is very different. The air at altitude is in a partial vacuum and the density is far less. Nikola Tesla had noted during his research into wireless energy transmission that it was preferable to transmit at altitude due to the better conductivity of air to high electrical frequencies. He states that the conductivity was "*better than copper wire*". This electrical conductivity of the air increases approximately exponentially with altitude.

The air is also electrically charged, as Wikipedia states: *Atmospheric electricity abounds in the environment; some traces of it are found less than four feet from the surface of the earth, but on attaining greater height it becomes more apparent. The main concept is that the air above the surface of the earth is usually, during fine weather, positively electrified, or at least that it is positive with respect to the Earth's surface, the Earth's surface being relatively negative.*

The measurements of atmospheric electricity can be seen as measurements of difference of potential between a point of the Earth's surface, and a point somewhere in the air above it. The atmosphere in different regions is often found to be at different local potentials, which differ from that of the ground sometimes even by as much as 3000 Volts within 100 feet (30 m).

Pressure is less and your body has to work harder to extract oxygen from the thinner air. The body will create extra blood cells and the blood will thicken. Everything in your body will start to expand as the pressure reduces. Your body is constantly working to address these expansion issues. You will need to be drinking plenty of water and electrolytes to enable the body to adapt. The opposite effects occur as you descend to lower elevations. Pressure changes are well known for their ability to make bones ache.

The humidity can either be extremely low if it is clear or extremely high if you are in the clouds.

As you can see, the environment at altitude is very different to what it is at sea level. For the purpose of human health, it appears that it is wise to work and live below 4,900 feet. Living and working above this altitude is likely to lead to altitude related health problems occurring. If you do work at altitude then daily commuting to altitude is undesirable and it is far better to stay there until your work is completed. You should probably not stay in a high altitude job for a long period of time and be aware that you are increasing your risks of illness, disease, cancer, and mental health problems in such jobs. Living or working near or above the tree line is not advisable.

You should only be living and working at altitude if you can trace your genetics to it. People in high cities such as La Paz, Bolivia, at an elevation of 11,942 ft will be genetically adapted to that area. For them, they would be wise to stay at that elevation.

Living at sea level may also be an issue today, particularly in or near to large coastal cities. Much of the pollution that is created by these will stay at sea level. The majority of pollutants are heavier than air and may stay near to the ground as they cool. This can be seen in large cities like Los Angeles as a cloud of pollution hanging over the city. It can also be seen near to erupting volcanoes.

If you live in locations such as these, it is advisable to live at an altitude that puts you above the pollution cloud. The ideal location for human health is not to live in such a polluted area.

"Because of the high altitude, you get drunk really fast. So everyone's drunk all the time."

Clea Duvall

Sounds & Vibrations

With the advent of wind turbines, sound and vibrations have started to receive the attention that they deserve. Extra low frequencies are now produced as part of modern society and they appear to be affecting some of the people that are exposed to them.

It is being widely reported that wind turbines are creating sounds and vibrations that can be sensed by people up to ten miles away! The book "Wind Turbine Syndrome" by Nina Pierpont MD PhD is reporting that people who live within two kilometers of wind turbines are reporting sickness that can be traced to the presence of these.

Dr. Nina Pierpont is reporting that similar symptoms also appear in humans near to natural gas compressor stations, industrial sewage pumping stations, and other power plants. Low frequency noise and infra-sound appear to be the problem.

Wind turbines that have been placed into the ocean will create frequencies and energy in the ocean that may upset the natural life there. It will be interesting to see the effects that these giants have on the long term ocean environment.

Living near busy roads and interstates may cause similar issues. A town that has an air-force base may have jets that go supersonic nearby. If so, you may find silent sonic boom infra-sound waves passing through your property. The supersonic airliner Concorde was famous for creating infra-sound that could be detected 200 miles away!

The Wikipedia article *"United States Navy in Vieques"* states: *In a study...48 of the 50 Vieques residents tested were diagnosed as suffering from vibroacoustic disease — a thickening of heart tissue caused by exposure to sonic booms. This disease is said to lead to heart arrhythmia, or even death.*

These sound waves that are created by modern society are carried on the wind and the direction of the wind will have a large impact on the noise that is created in the local environment daily.

Many people report their symptoms alleviate when they turn off fans in their homes and workplaces. This is because spinning fan blades can fill the surrounding area with infra-sound. I actually found that my air conditioning unit was mounted directly to the attic floor without any anti-vibration mounts. Such a system can induce infra-sound throughout the entire home!

You can easily make an infra-sound detector by opening a large window and placing a flexible sheet of clear acrylic up against the opening. Tack the three sides in place that are next to the frame to make them seal with the window frame. The side of the acrylic that is in the center of the window frame needs to be supported by a metal window screening bar that is flexible enough so that the wind can push the window and flex the acrylic pane. When infra-sound comes through from a supersonic jet or lightning, you will notice that the acrylic window will flex and vibrate.

When choosing a place to live, it makes sense not to be near industrial equipment and main roads. In the case of transportation systems, you will be getting subjected to the chemical pollution that they create also.

"The three great elemental sounds in nature are the sound of rain, the sound of wind in a primeval wood, and the sound of outer ocean on a beach."

Henry Beston

Chemical Exposure

Modern society is filled with chemicals that may be poisoning you. You are exposed to them almost everywhere you go. Here is a list of some of the things that you may want to avoid:

- Soaps.
- Shampoo and conditioners.
- Toothpaste.
- Mouthwash.
- Make up.
- Sunscreen.
- Lipstick.
- Nail varnish.
- Pesticides.
- Herbicides.
- Genetically modified foods.
- Processed foods.
- Medications.
- Exhaust emissions.
- Air fresheners.
- Scented candles.
- Stale air.
- Paint.
- Certain man-made materials.

If it is not natural, then you should be querying whether you should be exposing yourself to it. I recommend that you use organic versions of products where possible.

Many chemicals can cause photo-sensitivity to occur, as they can react with Sunlight. This can mislead you into thinking that you are allergic to the Sun. If you are having reactions to the Sun and you are sure that you are not sunlight deficient, then you should start to examine the chemicals on both the inside and outside of your body. These chemicals may be coming into you from the food and drinks that you are ingesting, and perhaps the air that you are breathing if you are near to air pollution.

Probably the only thing that should come into contact with your skin is natural clothing, natural materials (such as wood) and water. Avoid contact with plastics, synthetic fibers, metals, electronics, chemicals, soaps, make-up, and so on.

Multiple Chemical Sensitivity (MCS) is an emerging illness in the population and is caused by excessive exposure to chemicals. The documentary film "The Tomato Effect" by Faun Kime does a good job of explaining MCS and the corporate denials of its existence.

"You should keep human contact with man-made chemicals to a minimum."

Steven Magee

Society

"When machines and computers, profit motives and property rights are considered more important than people, the giant triplets of racism, materialism, and militarism are incapable of being conquered."
Martin Luther King

The society that you are born into can have major implications for your health. If you are born into a polluted industrial town, it is reasonable to expect that you will have illness in your childhood development that may linger with you for the rest of your life. If you are born into a natural rural environment with little modern development, then you will probably develop with few problems on the way to adulthood.

The more a society changes the natural environment to an industrialized environment then the more health problems that this will cause. Some of the problems that developing a natural environment with modern construction techniques can bring are:

- Loss of tree canopy.

- Loss or reduction of atmospheric DC voltage.

- Increased solar radiation power levels.

- Loss of nature modified solar radiation.

- Loss of ground vegetation.

- Loss of wild animal habitat and ecological systems.

- Loss of natural smells.

- Loss of natural pollen levels.

- Loss of natural sources of water.

- Loss of natural sources of food.

- Pollution.
- Crime.
- Lower quality of general health.
- Increased illness.
- Shorter or longer lifespan, depending on the pollution that you have been exposed to.
- The many man-made diseases of modern society:
  - Allergies.
  - Obesity.
  - Leukemia.
  - Diabetes.
  - Organ failure.
  - Cancer.
  - Aggression.
  - Depression.
  - Dementia.
  - Mental illness.
  - Electromagnetic Hypersensitivity (EHS).
  - Multiple Chemical Sensitivity (MCS).

Of course, no government official will ever tell you that the cities may be making the people in them ill. Nor will they tell you which professions have the shortest lifespans, increased rates of depression, or the highest illness, disease, cancer, and mental illness rates.

Talking about lifespans, some of the professions that appear to have poorer health and shorter lifespans than most are:

- Military.

- Police officer.

- Electrical line worker.

- Electrical switch yard worker.

- Communications field engineer.

- Power inverter field engineer.

- Pilot.

- Welder.

The next chart lists the most common professions for high rates of occupational deaths. When choosing a career, you should pay attention to statistics such as these.

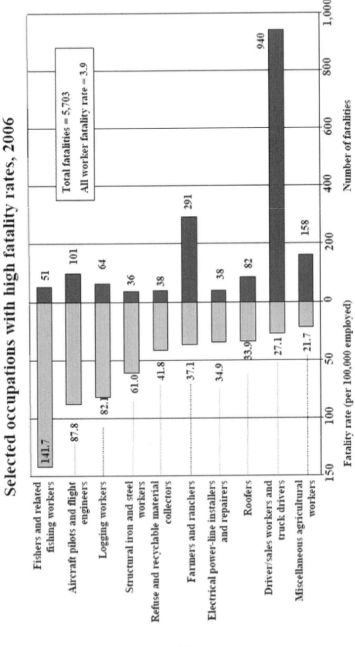

Selected occupations with high fatality rates, 2006

Total fatalities = 5,703
All worker fatality rate = 3.9

Number of fatalities

Fatality rate (per 100,000 employed)

Occupation	Number of fatalities	Fatality rate
Fishers and related fishing workers	51	141.7
Aircraft pilots and flight engineers	101	87.8
Logging workers	64	82.1
Structural iron and steel workers	36	61.0
Refuse and recyclable material collectors	38	41.8
Farmers and ranchers	291	37.1
Electrical power-line installers and repairers	38	34.9
Roofers	82	33.0
Driver/sales workers and truck drivers	940	27.1
Miscellaneous agricultural workers	158	21.7

It is interesting to note that for police officers, there is a well known observation of them which is called "Angry Aggression Theory"! As applied to police behavior, angry aggression theory argues that the chronic stress of police work along with the inability to respond to the actual sources of that stress increase both the perception of threats and the aggressiveness of responses to perceived threats. So what could be causing "Angry Aggression" in police officers? If you look at the above list you will see that they all have one thing in common: They all work in high electromagnetic radiation environments!

Dr. John Nash Ott proved the link between human health and electromagnetic interference (EMI) back in the 1950's in his book "My Ivory Cellar". Unfortunately, much of his work has been ignored, despite his attempts to get the government to research this area. It is of interest that although on the surface the government ignored the majority of Dr. John Nash Ott's work, they did go on to develop war weapons for the military that use EMI to inflict pain on the human body.

The cure for cancer will go down in history as the biggest government and corporate cover-up ever! As a result of Dr. John Nash Ott's work, cancer was well understood back in the 1950's and the covering up of both the cause and the cure for cancer has been part of the corporate and government culture since then. As Adrienne Rich says *"Lying is done with words and also with silence."* **This silence is well documented in the book "The Secret History of the War on Cancer" by Devra Davis.**

Time is one of the products of modern human society. When you examine time and how it relates to the cycles of nature, it appears to be a very flawed human concept. Most people are now working a forty hour week with ten days of vacation in the USA. The day starts at 8am and finishes at 5pm, Monday through to Friday. They are probably working in an office with electronic florescent lighting, computers, air conditioning, and energy star glass and, as such, they may be quite ill!

The problem with this is that the human mind and body does not function this way. The human mind and body is actually tied into the sunrise and the sunset for waking and sleeping. Therefore, in winter you may actually find yourself going to work in the dark and coming home in the dark! A very interesting concept for a creature that is not supposed to be awake before sunrise and should go to bed at sunset.

It is also a problem when it comes to the photosynthesis effects that take place within the human mind and body. If you are not exposing yourself to sunlight throughout the week then you may go into sunlight withdrawal. There are many people in modern society that are in some level of sunlight withdrawal and they do not realize it. It is commonly documented as Seasonal Affect Disorder (SAD) and causes a wide range of symptoms to appear during wintertime.

The really interesting thing is that there are many people who are in sunlight deficiency in the summertime! This can occur if you spend very little time outside during the week. In modern society this is a relatively easy state to fall into with the use of cars, homes, offices and indoor shopping. Walking to work or to the shops is becoming a thing of the past.

It is proposed that the correct work environment for the human should start no earlier than two hours after sunrise and finish no later than two hours before sunset. This would allow the human to revert back to its natural state of following the solar cycles for sleeping and waking periods.

The human addiction of using large amounts of energy to move humans and goods around should be stopped. A car is incredibly heavy and has a very inefficient engine. When you look at most people's jobs, they could easily be done from home. In an era of dwindling resources, one can only wonder about a society that requires its workers to commute daily to work by collectively burning massive amounts of fossil fuels. We should be moving towards a society that is local based in every aspect. Transportation of people and goods should be seen as a last resort and not the norm.

This use of fossil fuels is driven by governments that are heavily influenced by corporations. In the world of modern business and stock markets, a corporations success is determined by its profits. For corporations to make more profits, they need people to consume more. The modern governments encourage consumption to ensure that the corporations that fund their election campaigns continue to do so! It has been noticed by many that corporate donations and the corporate lobbying of the government has led to an arguably corrupt political system that works against the people and not for them.

A facet of this corruption is evidenced in the control of information to the masses. The mainstream media is now under the control of the corporations and they will select the information that is to be presented to the masses. Government media sources appear to be behaving in a similar fashion. An example of this was when the Fukushima nuclear power plant was venting radioactive steam into the environment in 2011 and the media was describing it as a *"harmless release of radiation"*! Who has ever heard of such a thing? The Fukushima nuclear complex went on to become the worst man-made engineering disaster in all of human history, outside of war.

Delivery of public information is now somewhat corrupted and once you become aware of this, it becomes hard to believe the information that is presented daily to the masses as "News". An example of this was the opening of Hoover Dam in the USA. Opened by the President of the USA as a wonderful achievement, in actuality, mistakes had been made in the construction of the project and it was quietly fixed over the following decade under a veil of secrecy. There have been many books written about the government's addiction to secrecy from their own people and "Secrets and Lies" by David Southwell is a good example of this. In 2011 the United States of America's Defense Secretary, Robert Gates, openly admitted that most governments lie.

As L. Neil Smith says *"I'm tired of being lied to by government, by the media, and by every corporation I have anything to do with."*

Wars have been prevalent in the last century and this should come as no surprise to those who understand the natural world. The modern human has destroyed its natural environment and created an extremely high man-made electromagnetic environment and a heavily polluted environment in general that creates corruption and aggression. Two-time Congressional Medal of Honor winner Maj. Gen. Smedley Butler had it right 75 years ago when he said of war: *"It is possibly the oldest, easily the most profitable, surely the most vicious [racket]...It is the only one in which the profits are reckoned in dollars and the losses in lives...It is conducted for the benefit of the very few, at the expense of the very many."*

There appears to have been a distortion of the truth regarding terrorism in the modern world. UNC sociology professor Charles Kurzman specializes in Middle East and Islamic studies, but he knows his American history too. *"Muslims are the latest wave of immigrants who are associated with acts of violence and are thought to be disloyal or not fully American, who are thought by many people to be impossible to integrate into American society. It was the same for the Irish in the 1840s, for Germans from the 1860s through World War I and for Italians who early in 20th Century were associated with anarchism and socialism and for Japanese Americans after Pearl Harbor,"* Kurzman said. Much of Kurzman's recent work has been to compile statistical profiles of Muslim Americans that reveal the majority of Muslim Americans are not the demons that some politicians and pundits have made them appear after 9-11.

Professor William Odom, formerly President Reagan's NSA Director wrote: *"As many critics have pointed, out, terrorism is not an enemy. It is a tactic. Because the United States itself has a long record of supporting terrorists and using terrorist tactics, the slogans of today's war on terrorism merely makes the United States look hypocritical to the rest of the world."*

The cost of the 9-11 attacks through to the Bin Laden assassination is estimated at 3 trillion dollars, the United States of America is heavily in debt, unemployment is high and many large corporations do not pay taxes. It is clear that something has gone wrong in the government system! Martin Luther King had it right when he said *"Our scientific power has outrun our spiritual power. We have guided missiles and misguided men."*

The history that is now being taught to many school children is somewhat distorted. The government writes and carefully selects the information that children are to be taught from and one can only wonder why the events are not entirely accurately portrayed in the history books that they use. There are many books that discuss this concept and "Lies My Teacher Told Me: Everything Your American History Textbook Got Wrong." by James W. Loewen is one example of this.

Children are now raised to "get a job" instead of enjoying childhood. If we look at traditional rural cultures, children are raised by their families through to adulthood. School does not exist and the teaching is from father to son. What child really aspires to go to school and get a job? Most children I know want to spend time with their families and friends. Being educated by strangers in a school that is miles away from their home is generally not high in their priorities. Separating children from their families in an effort to educate them for incorporation into an industrial machine is a flawed social policy.

Capitalism has shown its true colors in the energy industry. Labeling toxic processes as "clean and green", such as coal, gas, and nuclear energy is a very clear case of "Green-washing". It is clearly not true! The energy industry branding itself as clean and green is possibly one of the biggest lies ever told to the population. The lie is needed to keep the Industrial Revolution going at the expense of the mass population, nature and ultimately, the Earth. Capitalism appears to be following a policy of lie, confuse and deny in order to keep economic expansion progressing. As Upton Sinclair observed *"It is difficult to get a man to understand something when his job depends on not understanding it."*

It appears that capitalism has reached the lose-lose situation. The continued expansion of the destruction of natural systems to provide for the consumption for an ever increasing world population will lead to human extinction as

the natural systems become more polluted. They will all start to shut down, leaving humanity stranded with no further options. As Gandhi said *"The Earth provides enough to satisfy every man's need, but not every man's greed."*

Future historians will regard the era of capitalism as a disease of an insane mind. Unfortunately, the modern human is so badly polluted from the destruction of its own environment that it thinks the current situation is completely normal!

The longer climate change is ignored by modern governments and ineffective policies are followed, the bigger the task of effective change becomes. Lester R. Brown has recognized this in his book "Plan B 4.0: Mobilizing to Save Civilization". Change could have been easily effected back in the 1950's by governments to prevent the situation that we find ourselves in today. As each year passes, little changes and everything becomes more polluted. It is clear that continued expansion and pollution is a path to the collective suicide of humanity. At the point where the mass population realizes exactly how serious the situation is, it will require more effort than all of the wars put together to effect change, assuming that it is not too late to change at that time.

Reform for the people and by the people is required to prevent humanity from pursuing the path to extinction. A switch from focusing on profits to that of the future generation's inheritance is needed, as we are the keepers of the Earth. I am personally ashamed of the inheritance that has been left by my generation. The next generation has a huge task ahead of them.

The following books would be good further reading on this subject:

- "Why Leaders Lie: The Truth About Lying in International Politics." by John J. Mearsheimer.

- "Political Ponerology: A Science on the Nature of Evil Adjusted for Political Purposes." by Andrzej M. Lobaczewski.

- "Denialism: How Irrational Thinking Harms the Planet and Threatens our Lives." by Michael Specter.

- "Sparking a Worldwide Energy Revolution: Social Struggles in the Transition to a Post Petrol World." by Kolya Abramsky.

- "The Transition Handbook: From Oil Dependancy to Local Resilience." by Rob Hopkins.

"The price good men pay for indifference to public affairs is to be ruled by evil men."

Plato

Summary

The value of nature to humanity is infinite. There has been a lack of understanding of the functions that nature provides to humanity that is clearly instinctively present in young children and native people. This lack of understanding has led to widespread illness, disease, cancer, and mental health issues in the modern population.

The destruction and detachment from the natural environment that the modern human has displayed will be regarded as one of the biggest mistakes ever made in human history. The pollution of the atmosphere, rivers and oceans is already acknowledged as an environmental catastrophe that has led to the extinction of millions of species.

It is common to see headlines that underline the failing modern society, such as *"Diabetes Rate Doubles"* or *"UK Depression Rate Up by 40%"*. Diabetes and depression are modern diseases born out of the Industrial Revolution, as are so many of the modern diseases. It is quite a simple progression to where we are today:

- Cutting the trees down significantly increased the ground based radiation levels that the human was exposed to. It also removed the tree canopy that has a DC voltage on it. This led to an increase in illness and disease. This appears to be the start of widespread mental illness in the human race.

- The adoption of electricity led to the regular exposure of electromagnetic interference in the human body. This corresponded to another increase in illness, disease, cancer, and mental health issues. New illnesses and diseases were born with the progression of electricity. Many babies became too large to fit through the birth canal.

- Drinking incorrect water and eating poor quality food has caused many health conditions to occur.

- Allowing the human mind and body to atrophy has opened up the human to many illnesses and diseases that were not present before the adoption of sedentary lifestyles.

- The continued pollution of the atmosphere, rivers, and oceans is increasing human illness, disease, cancer, and mental health issues, and the continuation of this process should be expected to lead to human extinction.

Illness, disease, cancer, mental health issues and altered growth rates in babies and children are the current fruits of modern society. There is no mystery about cancer, it is the disease of pollution. Unfortunately, when it comes to pollution and human health, cancer is just the tip of the iceberg. Without the environment, we are all dead.

I have every expectation that in the future, electricity will be regarded in the same way that asbestos and smoking are viewed today. The electrification of the ground that we walk on can only be described as the actions of an insane race of people. Stray voltage effects, biological field coupling, toxic artificial lighting products and willingly electrifying the air with radio and microwaves will be documented by future historians as the peak of human insanity. Indeed, the historical records indicate that Nikola Tesla, the inventor of many of the modern systems that we routinely use, may have been one of the earliest documented cases of environmental and electromagnetic hypersensitivity!

The most polluted animal on the planet today is the modern human.

It is time to change back to a nature based society and put the Industrial Revolution behind us as an unfortunate mistake in human history. Never again should we have nations whose measure of success is how much money they can make. Rather, nations should be using nature based standards to gauge their success. There should be no higher standard than the health and well-being of their children and their elderly people.

Nature is well documented as bringing about positive health and mental well being. Research findings include:

- Better cognitive functioning.
- More self discipline and impulse control.
- Greater overall mental health.
- Enhanced recovery from surgery.
- Enable and support higher levels of physical activity.
- Improved immune system functioning.
- Improved memory.

Less access to nature is linked to:

- Exacerbated attention deficit/hyperactivity disorder symptoms.
- Higher rates of anxiety disorders.
- Higher rates of clinical depression.
- Greater rates of childhood obesity.
- Higher rates of overall disease.
- Higher rates of mortality in younger and older adults.

Here is what appears to be the recipe for good human health:

- Drinking hot tea made with hard mineralized water.
- Fresh air in a natural outdoor environment.

- Fresh organic food of mainly fruits and vegetables.

- Daily high activity strength exercises.

- No industrial sound or vibration waves.

- An outdoor solar radiation environment that is modified by the tree canopy.

- An annual hibernation cycle.

- Correct daily exposure to solar radiation.

- Exposure to the natural DC atmospheric voltage.

- No unnatural electromagnetic interference (EMI) effects.

- No man-made chemicals.

- A supportive social structure that recognizes and promotes the beneficial effects that nature is providing to the human mind and body.

Energy fields define who we are as humans. If you are in environments that are creating positive energy, then you will have excellent mental and physical health. If you are in environments where the energy levels are negative, then you will fall into poor mental and physical health. Unfortunately, today's modern society has created far more negative energy fields and finding good mental and physical health is becoming increasingly difficult.

Feng Shui is the study of positive energy in the human environment. It literally means wind and water. The people who developed Feng Shui understood that human emotions and health were governed by their environments. If you are feeling ill or having emotional issues, you should apply the science of Feng Shui to your environment as it will probably help a lot. You cannot go wrong by having an environment that has the science of Feng Shui applied to it.

I never thought that I would be using my Red Cross and St. Johns medical training, biomedical background, astronomical skills and my electrical & electronic engineering degree that I obtained in my twenties to fix the health problems that showed up in my thirties. My skills turned out to be very useful, far more effective than any doctor I saw. I do find it rather strange that to live in modern society that I have to behave like I am on the International Space Station! This lifestyle underscores how alien the modern human environment has become.

The book "Harmony" by the Prince of Wales has provided an excellent road map back to where we need to be. Harmony with nature has always been known to be the way to live a long, natural, pain-free, and healthy life.

I hope that you enjoyed the book and I wish you the very best of health.

"Every human being is the author of his own health or disease."

Sivanada

References

- Bell Hooks.
- Bill Gates.
- Clea Duvall.
- Deepak Chopra.
- Do Trees Strengthen Urban Communities, Reduce Domestic Violence? Paper by By W. C. Sullivan, Ph.D. & Frances E. Kuo, Ph.D.
- Dr. George Crile.
- Dr. Jim Burch: http://cpcp.sph.sc.edu/fs/burch.htm
- Dr. John Nash Ott: http://www.biolightgroup.com/Ott.html
- Dr. Magda Havas: http://www.magdahavas.com/
- Dr. Philip Stoddard: http://www2.fiu.edu/~stoddard/
- Dr. Samuel Milham MD MPH: http://www.sammilham.com/
- Dr. William Rae: http://www.ecopolitan.com/dr-william-rae
- Earthing: The Most Important Health Discovery Ever? by Clinton Ober, Stephen T. Sinatra and Martin Zucker: http://earthinginstitute.net/
- Edward Stanley.
- Electrocution of America: Is Your Utility Company Out to Kill You? by Russ Allen.
- Elizabeth Kelley MA, Director of the Electromagnetic Safety Alliance.
- Eric Schmidt.
- Francis Bacon.

- Frank Lloyd Wright.
- Frederick Douglass.
- Freeman Dyson.
- Galileo Galilei.
- Google Maps: http://maps.google.com
- Henry Beston.
- Henry St. John.
- John F. Kennedy.
- Joyce Carol Oates.
- Leonardo da Vinci.
- Les Brown.
- Light, Radiation, and You - How to Stay Healthy by Dr. John N. Ott.
- Marilyn vos Savant.
- Martin Luther King.
- myfoxny.com article *America's anger epidemic: why?*
- Patrick Swayze.
- Plan B 4.0: Mobilizing to Save Civilization by Lester R. Brown.
- Plato.
- Popular Science: http://www.popsci.com/science/article/2010-02/disconnected
- Sivanada.
- Stetzer Electric: http://www.stetzerelectric.com/
- Ted Scambos.
- Tom Stoppard.

- UNC Terrorism Research:
  http://www.unc.edu/spotlight/terrorism_research
- Virginia Woolf.
- William Wordsworth.
- Wikipedia: http://www.wikipedia.org/

"None of us is as smart as all of us."
Eric Schmidt

Internet

Manufacturers of ultraviolet (UV) transmitting full spectrum acrylic window glazing sheets are:

Lucite International, Inc: LuciteLux UTRAN UVT:
http://www.lucitelux.com/product.aspx?productID=4

Spartech: Solacryl "Monkey-Shine" SUVT:
http://www.spartech.com/polycast/Spartech-Polycast-Solacryl-Monkey-Shine.pdf

Vitamin D Wiki is a useful collection of vitamin D information:
http://vitamindwiki.com/VitaminDWiki

Useful electromagnetic websites are:

Bioinitiative Report is a rationale for biologically-based public exposure standards for electromagnetic fields (ELF and RF):
http://www.bioinitiative.org/

Dr. Magda Havas, PhD, co-author of "Public Health SOS: The Shadow Side of the Wireless Revolution":
http://www.magdahavas.com/

Dr. Nina Pierpont is developing the health effects of wind turbines and infrasound: http://www.windturbinesyndrome.com/

Dr. Samuel Milham, author of "Dirty Electricity":

http://www.sammilham.com/

ElectroSensitivity UK is a website that aims to provide unbiased and balanced information to help those who have become sensitive to mobile and cordless phones, their masts, WiFi, and a multitude of common everyday electrical appliances: http://www.es-uk.info/

Environmental Health Center-Dallas, Texas, medically tests and treats human health problems including sensitivities to pollens, molds, dust, foods, chemicals, air (indoor/outdoor), water, electromagnetic sensitivity (EMF), and many more health problems as they relate to our environment: http://www.ehcd.com/

Environmental Radiation LLC offers the services to identify the modern invisible toxins that we are routinely exposed to and the know-how to rectify the problems.

http://www.environmentalradiation.com/

FEB - The Swedish Association for the ElectroHyperSensitive:

http://www.feb.se/index_int.htm

Guidelines of the Austrian Medical Association for the diagnosis and treatment of EMF related health problems and illnesses (EMF syndrome)

http://freiburger-appell-2012.info/media/EMF%20Guideline %20OAK-AG%20%202012%2003%2003.pdf

Less EMF are a leading supplier in the USA of electromagnetic radiation products: http://www.lessemf.com/

Mast-Victims.org - An international community website for people suffering adverse health effects from mobile phone masts in the vicinity of their homes

http://www.mast-victims.org/

Medical Perspective on Environmental Sensitivities - Canadian Human Rights Commission: http://www.chrc-ccdp.gc.ca/sites/default/files/envsensitivity_en.pdf

Powerwatch UK: http://www.powerwatch.org.uk/

Smart Meter Opposition Groups in the United States of America: http://www.takebackyourpower.net/directory/us/

Stetzer Electric, Inc, manufacturers of the STETZERiZER® Filter:

http://www.stetzerelectric.com/

WEEP - The Canadian initiative to stop wireless, electric, and electromagnetic pollution: http://www.weepinitiative.org/

World Health Organization (WHO) International Workshop on Electromagnetic Field Hypersensitivity: http://www.who.int/peh-emf/publications/reports/EHS_Proceedings_June2006.pdf

"The Internet is becoming the town square for the global village of tomorrow."

Bill Gates

<u>Acknowledgments</u>

This book was influenced by:

- My father for his discussions about how the fat content in meat changes color between diary cows and open range cows.

- Claudia Sandoval M.S.W. for her wisdom on trees and how it relates in the social environment.

- My neighbors for their understanding and assistance with my biological experiments.

- Dr. John Nash Ott for his extensive research into health, light, and radiation. His lasting legacy of publications was a wonderful gift to the next generation:

  - My Ivory Cellar; [the story of time-lapse photography].

  - Health and Light: The Extraordinary Study That Shows How Light Affects Your Health and Emotional Well Being.

  - Light, Radiation, and You: How to Stay Healthy.

  - Color and Light: Their Effects on Plants, Animals and People.

  - Exploring the Spectrum: The Effects of Natural and Artificial Light on Living Organisms.

- The numerous people and companies who are referenced in this book that have worked diligently to bring the important science of environmental health to the masses.

"Help others achieve their dreams and you will achieve yours."

Les Brown

About the Author

Steven started his career at one of the largest university research and teaching hospitals in Europe. Working in the electrical engineering group, he obtained a Bachelors with Honors in Electrical and Electronic Engineering. Human health was a strong draw and he moved into the biomedical team, serving the regions hospitals. During this time he developed a fascination for human illness and disease and the causes of it, many of which were not understood.

He joined the Isaac Newton Group of Telescopes in 1999 and went to live in La Palma. La Palma is part of the Canary Islands, governed by Spain. During this time he worked with the leading European astronomers and developed his astronomical and optics skills. He became fluent in Spanish and their culture.

In 2001 he became a Chartered Electrical Engineer and joined the W. M. Keck Observatory in Hawaii. This was the world's leading astronomical facility and home to the world's two largest segmented mirror telescopes. Steven developed segmented optics and interferometry skills while working alongside world leading astronomers. During this time Steven constructed his own off-grid solar powered home in the last of the traditional Hawaiian fishing villages in Miloli'i, Hawaii. He learned Hawaiian Pidgin English and the Hawaiian culture during his time there.

In 2006, Steven became the Director of the MDM Observatory in Sells, Arizona, USA. Working for Columbia University and later, Dartmouth College, he developed the facility to modern standards. He learned an appreciation of the native Americans and their culture from the Tohono O'odham Nation.

In 2008, Steven joined the solar power revolution that was sweeping the USA and commissioned the largest CIGS thin film solar photovoltaic installation in the world.

A year later he commissioned the largest solar photovoltaic power plant in the USA. The system rated power was quoted as 25,000,000 watts AC with over 90,500 solar modules that were mounted to 158 single-axis tracker systems in three hundred acres of land.

He went on to develop the solar photovoltaic team for a large international company.

In 2010 he started to research radiation and publish the leading books on the subject.

"All truths are easy to understand once they are discovered; the point is to discover them."

Galileo Galilei

Author Contact

I hope that you found the book informative and please let me know about any questions or comments about the book. I can be contacted through the StevenMageeBooks channel on www.youtube.com.

I am a consultant in the areas that I research at Environmental Radiation LLC and please feel free to contact me for any help or assistance. This is the website:

http://www.environmentalradiation.com/

You can follow the twitter feed at:

Steven Magee @EnvironmentEMR

The Facebook page is:

https://www.facebook.com/EnvironmentEMR

You may find my other books useful:

Solar Photovoltaic

- **Complete Solar Photovoltaics for Residential, Commercial, and Utility Systems:** Steven Magee has combined his three top selling books on solar power systems into one edition. Complete Solar Photovoltaics will train you on solar photovoltaics and show you how to design grid connected solar photovoltaic power systems. Operations and maintenance is detailed to enable you to have a complete understanding of solar photovoltaics from start to finish.

- **Solar Photovoltaics for Consumers, Utilities, and Investors:** This book details solar photovoltaic systems for consumers, utilities and investors. This would encompass residential, commercial and utility systems that are connected to the utility grid. There is a discussion of the different technologies available for the consumer and their advantages and disadvantages. For the utilities, there is invaluable advice on planning and constructing large projects. For the investor, forward looking statements try to predict the future of solar photovoltaics.

- **Solar Photovoltaic Training for Residential, Commercial, and Utility Systems:** This book details solar photovoltaic training for those who are interested in this area and also for those who are already working in the field. This would encompass residential, commercial, and utility systems that are connected to the utility grid. It is a comprehensive overview of a rapidly growing world of solar photovoltaic power generation technology.

- **Solar Photovoltaic Design for Residential, Commercial, and Utility Systems:** This book details how to design reliable solar photovoltaic power generation systems from a residential system, progressing to a commercial system, and finishing at the largest utility power generation systems. By following the guidelines in this book and your local solar photovoltaic electrical codes, you will be able to design trouble free solar power systems that give many years of reliable operation. When designed well, solar photovoltaic power generation is an excellent source of electrical power that results in much lower electricity bills, the power company will even refund you for the excess energy generated by your system if it is large enough. Building a grid tied solar power system is a relatively easy task. Given the large amount of government and electrical utility financial incentives that are available, it is a great time to join in the solar power revolution that is taking place in the world today.

- **Solar Photovoltaic Operation and Maintenance for Residential, Commercial, and Utility Systems:** This book details how to operate and maintain residential, commercial, and utility solar photovoltaic systems that are connected to the utility grid. By following the guidelines in this book you will be able to operate and maintain solar power systems that should give many years of reliable operation. Invaluable trouble shooting advice will aid in returning your system to full operation in the event of a problem.

- **Solar Photovoltaic DC Calculations for Residential, Commercial, and Utility Systems:** This book details how to run calculations for the DC circuit of solar photovoltaic systems. This would encompass residential, commercial, and utility systems that are connected to the utility grid. It covers the range of conditions that solar photovoltaic modules are exposed to throughout the year and shows how to incorporate these into an effective DC circuit that is well designed and reliable.

- **Solar Photovoltaic Resource for Residential, Commercial, and Utility Systems:** This book is a resource of information that is used in the solar photovoltaic field. This would encompass residential, commercial, and utility systems that are connected to the utility grid. It is a comprehensive collection of notes, diagrams, pictures and charts for a rapidly growing world of solar photovoltaic power generation technology. This book is illustrated in color.

Solar

- **Solar Irradiance and Insolation for Power Systems:** This book is a resource of information that is used in the solar power generation field. This would encompass residential, commercial, and utility systems that are connected to the utility grid. It is a comprehensive collection of notes, diagrams, pictures, and charts for a rapidly growing world of solar photovoltaic power generation technology. This book is illustrated in color.

- **Solar Site Selection for Power Systems:** This book is a comprehensive collection of images, diagrams, and notes that document the effects of light and heat in the solar power generation field. This would encompass residential, commercial, and utility systems that are connected to the utility grid. This is essential information for a rapidly growing world of solar power generation technology. This book is illustrated in color.

Architecture

- **Solar Reflections for Architects, Engineers, and Human Health:** This book is a comprehensive collection of images, diagrams, and notes that document the effects of sunlight in architecture. This is essential information for architects, engineers, and the medical profession. The discovery of the "Multiple-Sun" effect in architecture is detailed and this book is illustrated in color.

Human Health

- **Solar Radiation – A Cause of Illness and Cancer?** Illness and cancers have become part of our modern culture. It has been discovered that extremely high levels of man-made solar radiation exist in modern society. Could this be the one of the causes of illness and cancers? This book examines the increase in solar radiation and applies it to human health.

- **Solar Radiation, Global Warming, and Human Disease:** This book examines the modern development of the Earth and the potential impacts on global warming and human disease. The destruction of the forests for modern agricultural use appears to have effects that are not fully understood and these are explored. Radiation deficiency and radiation overloading are investigated to see if they are factors in many illnesses and diseases.

- **Toxic Light:** Toxic Light takes a look at the light pollution that may be in your local environment and relates it to the health problems that it may cause. Light in the human environment is only just starting to be understood and something as innocent as your sunglasses may be able to make you ill! There are many examples of commonplace items in your environment that may have the ability to affect your health. Get ready for enlightenment about the most important human nutrient of light!

- **Toxic Health:** Toxic Health takes a look at the pollution that may be in your local environment and relates it to the health problems that it can cause. Pollution in the human environment is only just starting to be understood and something as innocent as light may be able to make you really ill! There are many examples of commonplace items in your environment that may have the ability to affect your health. In particular, we will investigate if modern city life is the most toxic thing of all to the modern human!

- **Toxic Electricity:** Random aches and pains? Fatigue? Insomnia? Facial pains? Irregular heartbeats? Sick kids? Relationship problems? Blotchy skin? Anxiety? Toxic electricity takes a look at the electrical system and asks the question: Is this one of the most toxic endeavors that humanity has ever engaged in?

Forensics

- **Electrical Forensics:** Electrical Forensics examines the many aspects of electricity, electronics and wireless communications that may lead to unusual behaviors to occur in humans. Electromagnetic interference is well known for its ability to affect mental functioning and human health. Electrical Forensics demonstrates how to identify toxic electromagnetic environments that may be the root cause of accidents and crimes.

- **Health Forensics:** Health Forensics examines the many aspects of modern society that may lead to unusual behaviors to occur in humans. Modern society has adopted habits that are well known for their ability to affect mental functioning and human health. Health Forensics demonstrates how to identify toxic human environments that may be the root cause of accidents and crimes.

Religion

- **Solar Radiation, the Book of Revelations, and the Era of Light – Part 1:** Welcome to the Era of Light! Light has long been known to be essential nourishment for the human body. We will explore the different types of light that are present on Earth and relate it to human health and nature. Light is discussed extensively in the Bible and we will see if we can associate our findings to it. Finally, we will investigate if the Industrial Revolution has created the ultimate toxin of poisonous sunlight!

Professional

- **Engineering Science and Education Journal Volume: 11, Issue: 4, Active Control Systems for Large Segmented Optical Mirrors:** A new generation of optical telescopes is on the drawing board. These will be true giants with primary mirrors having a diameter of up to 100 meters. The technology that will enable this revolution to take place was developed at the W. M. Keck Observatory in Hawaii, where the world's largest segmented mirrors are in daily use. This article looks at how the W. M. Keck Observatory proved the mirror technology that will be behind this new generation of telescopes.

You can search "Steven Magee Books" for the very latest publications.

www.youtube.com videos supporting the ideas in the books can be found by searching: StevenMageeBooks

"Life-transforming ideas have always come to me through books."

Bell Hooks

Book Reviews

Electrical Forensics rated 5 out of 5 stars.

Review by John Puccetti on October 27, 2013 titled "Dangers of electricity"

Steven has made many of the health problems of our century known in his book. But what will we do is this information? We live in a corporate dictatorship that masquerades as democracy.

Toxic Electricity rated 5 out of 5 stars.

Review by Sam Wieder on December 13, 2013 titled "A Most Illuminating, Educational, and Helpful Book"

Toxic Electricity provides a clear and comprehensive description of the many ways in which electrical fields impact human health and offers simple steps that anyone can take to live a more vibrant life in our electrically toxic world. The author does a masterful job of presenting some fairly complex concepts in a way that is easily understandable. Reading this book will give you a deeper understanding of how unseen radiation in your living and working environment may be impacting you. If you've been battling different health challenges or are chronically tired for no apparent reason, this book may very well open your eyes to some answers that will help you regain your health and your life.

Peter Sullivan @petermsullivan9 twittered on 10th December 2013:

@EnvironmentEMR Thanks for writing about the #autism / #EMF theory in you book Toxic Electricity. Also love the use of plants as "canaries".

Toxic Electricity: Eric Van rated it 5 out of 5 stars on Dec 23, 2012

If you think that you're home or work environment is safe and sound think again. If you are fatigued or have strange ailments currently or are concerned about cancer in the future then I recommend reading this book and getting an education into how you can avoid the toxins you receive from electricity.

Toxic Light rated 4 out of 5 Stars.

Review by John Puccetti on January 2, 2014 titled "Very technical".

I recommend you read "Tesla a man out of time" before you read this book. It is hard to grasp how much is wrong with radio frequencies and the electric grid and smart meters unless you really do some research first. But it is a wake up call to us all. Well worth reading.

"A good, sympathetic review is always a wonderful surprise."

Joyce Carol Oates

35822195R00150

Made in the USA
Lexington, KY
25 September 2014